The Ultimate Asia Train Travel Guide

A BlueMarbleXpress Explore the World Vacation Series

by J. Doyle White

Table of Contents

Introduction

Asia is the biggest continent on Earth, a continent which brings together such contrasts and incredible attractions that one lifetime doesn't seem enough to capture its beauty and vast culture. It covers 8.7% of the entire surface of our planet and is home to over 60% of the Globe's population. The borders of this continent are still pretty hard to determine but, in general terms, we could say that Asia stretches from the mountains that rise proudly around the Black Sea in the west to Siberia and its unfriendly climate. In the east you can discover the Pacific Ocean, while to the south lays the Indian Ocean. Australia comes to complete the painting by bordering Asia to the southeast.

From the highest point of Asia, which is Mount Everest, to the Dead Sea, the lowest point, Asia amazes and fascinates.

Traveling by train is probably the easiest way to get a chance to admire its sceneries without having to worry about traffic or find the right directions. Asia seems created for being discovered by train and, although the railroad arrived here around 1800s, today Asia manages to have one of the best train systems in the world and to be a destination for luxurious trains like the Eastern & Oriental Express and the Indian Maharaja - Deccan Odyssey.

The most famous railway in the world is undoubtedly the Trans-Siberian. The Trans-Siberian train's journey starts in Moscow—the capital of Russia—and ends in Vladivostok, where you can take a ferry to get to Niigata, a city in Japan. The railway is about 9,000 km and the journey is accompanied by spectacular sceneries. A complete trip lasts 6 days—6 days of wonder and beauty.

The project for the Trans-Asia railway started in the 1960s. When finished, it will cover about 80,000 km of railway and cross 27 countries in South-East Asia, North-East Asia, Central Asia and Caucasus, South Asia, Iran, and Turkey. Trans-Asia railway has as final goal of linking Istanbul to Singapore and also adding corridors to China, the central states in Asia, and Russia. Currently, the only railroads that are functional connect Turkey to Iran, and China and Iran to Central Asia. The Bosphorus Tunnel was opened in 2013 and it connects the European and Asian sides of Istanbul.

Until the Trans-Asia railway will be finished, let's enjoy the available railroads and discover the wonders of Asia by train.

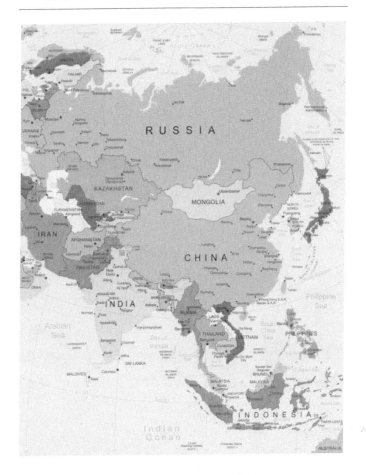

Discover the Most Fascinating Attractions in Asia

Asia is home to countries like Japan, China, Thailand, India, and Russia. Therefore, visitors will discover an infinite number of spectacular attractions unseen in any other places of the world. If you plan your itinerary wisely, you will be able to admire many of Asia's attractions right from the comfort of your train cabin.

Boracay Island, Philippines

Boracay is a small island situated about 196 miles away from Manila. Despite its reduced size, this island is among the most beautiful islands in the world. Every year, Boracay Beach receives awards from different publications and it is a constant dream destination for people all over the world. If serenity ever had its picture taken, it would definitely resemble Boracay Island. The easiest way to get there is by plane. It will take you about one hour to go from Manila to Caticlan, where you can take a ferry to paradise. The trip lasts about 10 minutes.

Chocolate Hills, Philippines

Chocolate lovers, hold it together! We're not talking about actual chocolate hills, but about some hills in the Bohol Province of Philippines that, during the dry season, become really brown. From a glance it seems like a chocolate scenery and a dream come true for those who love this treat. Looking closer, you can see that they are natural cone-shaped hills, with heights between 98 to 390 feet, made from grass-covered limestone. No one knows how they were formed and why they cover over 20 square miles. So they are not only very attractive, but also mysterious: the perfect combination for an attraction to become among the most visited in the area.

Forbidden City, China

The Forbidden City is situated in the center of Beijing and, for almost 500 years, was the imperial palace of Chinese Emperors. Don't expect to see one of the imperial palaces you're used to. This is more of a complex or city than a simple palace. It has 980 buildings that cover over 170 acres, and it is home to hundreds of priceless treasures and artifacts. This palace-fortress became a UNESCO World Heritage Site in 1987, and it is one of the must-see attractions during a trip to Beijing.

Gobi Desert, Mongolia

The Gobi Desert, which covers a surface of over 500,000 square miles, is not as deserted as some may think. It has an impressive number of eco-systems and is home to many animal species, from camels and gazelles to snow leopards (exactly, snow!). During summer, the temperatures reach up to 50 degrees Celsius (122 degrees Fahrenheit), while during the cold months they can drop as low as -40 degrees Celsius (-40 degrees Fahrenheit). A little bit extreme and moody for a desert area.

Great Wall of China

Everybody knows the Great Wall of China. Even the aliens have a chance to admire it from space. The Great Wall of China was built more than 2,000 years ago, but it is still going strong and famous. It is 9,000 km long and definitely one of the wonders of the world. Tourists have access to only 10 km of the entire length, but this section is enough for anyone to be overwhelmed by the grandeur of this construction.

Ha Long Bay, Vietnam

Ha Long Bay is an absolutely enchanting bay in Vietnam, famous among tourists who visit these parts of the world. It has a surreal beauty and a serenity that can calm even a hurricane. The bay is dominated by almost 2,000 monolithic limestone islands covered in vegetation. Some of the islands are inhabited by people who have fishing and aquaculture as main occupations. The bay is situated in the north-eastern part of Vietnam, more specifically in the Quang Ninh Province.

Huangguoshu Waterfall, China

If you love spectacular sceneries, then you should definitely admire the Huangguoshu Waterfall National Park. The park is situated 45 km away from Anshun City, China. Once you get there, you will get a once-in-a-lifetime chance to admire one of the largest waterfalls in China. The waterfall is 77.8 meters tall and 101 meters wide. There are some tourist spots where you can capture the beauty of the waterfall. You can choose the Waterfall-Viewing Pavilion, to admire the waterfall from a distance, or the Water-Viewing Stage, to get a chance to discover the waterfall from a bird's point of view.

Jigokudani Monkey Park, Japan

Jigokudani Monkey Park is home to some pretty pretentious Japanese Macaque monkeys that just love to relax in the hot and steamy waters of the Jigokudani Valley. The park is situated in Yamanouchi, Nagano Prefecture, and is accessible by a 2 km trail that crosses a forest. The Snow Monkeys, how they are also known, come down for their jacuzzi sessions during winter. In the warmer months, they can be seen all around the park.

Kampung Kuantan Fireflies, Malaysia

This attraction is not about a mysterious city or an unseen sight. This attraction is about a fairy tale setting where an infinite number of fireflies get together and light up the night. The "Pteroptyx Tener" fireflies can be admired during a trip to Kuala Selangor, more exactly the Kuantan village. The only way you can get closer to these fireflies (they are actually 6 mm long beetles) is by a boat, which the locals call "sampan" (small boat). A boat can carry 4 passengers maximum, and tickets can be purchased at the information center. The scenery will remind you of a magical Christmas card.

K2 Mountain, Pakistan

It seems that Asia is not only home to the highest mountain on Earth, but also to the second highest mountain, K2. K2 can be found in the Himalayas, the Pakistan section. Its peak is situated at an altitude of 8,611 meters above sea level, and hundreds of travelers around the world have dared to climb it and admire the planet from above. Also called the Savage Mountain, K2 is such a dangerous mountain that one of four mountaineers who climbs it dies trying to reach its peak.

Mount Everest

Mount Everest is the highest mountain in the world, reaching up to 8,848 meters above sea level. Mount Everest is situated exactly at the border between China and Nepal, in the Mahalangur section of the Himalaya Mountains. As expected, the highest mountain of our planet attracted and still attracts many mountaineers eager to get on top of the world and admire what is probably one of the most breathtaking sceneries a human can see. There are two main climbing routes, one from Nepal and one from Tibet.

Mount Fuji, Japan

The tallest mountain in Japan is definitely worthy of your time and admiration. If you want to see an almost perfect symmetrical volcanic cone that dominates the surrounding area, then you should plan a trip to Mount Fiji. The mountain is so spectacular that, on a clear day, it can be seen even from Tokyo. The mountain has an altitude of 3,776 m. It is one of the favorite destinations for hikers from around the world that arrive eager to get on its peak.

Natural Forest Park of Zhangjiaje, China

One of the natural wonders of Asia, the Natural Forest Park of Zhangjiaje, seems a surreal painting. A UNESCO World Heritage Site, this park is home to some of the weirdest—and at the same time the most incredible—rock formations. The Hallelujah Mountains, as they are called, seem like have just fallen from the sky and decided to remain in the Hunan Province of China. A trip to this attraction guarantees the WOW effect and unique pictures for your Facebook page.

Pak Ou Caves, Laos

The Pak Ou Caves on Mekong River are one of the natural wonders of Asia. The Tham Ting (lower cave) and Tham Theung (upper cave) are situated right where the Mekong River meets the Nam Ou River, 15 miles from the Luang Prabang city. Nature carved them from a limestone cliff and offered them an unseen beauty. Today, these caves are a Buddhist shrine and house thousands of Buddha statues and carvings.

Sigiriya, Sri Lanka

Once the capital of King Kasypa, Sigiriya is today one of the most visited historical attractions in Sri Lanka and a UNESCO World Heritage Site. The scenery is dominated by a marvelous 650 feet monolith, also known as the "Lion Rock," that rises up from a forested plain. This is a clear reminder that no one can understand the way nature likes to work. Sigirya is situated in the Matale District, Central Province of Sri Lanka, and is connected to the city of Dambulla by bus.

Taj Mahal, India

One of the most famous attractions in the world, the Taj Mahal, is situated in Agra, Uttar Pradesh. Taj Mahal was built between 1631 and 1648, as a tomb for the wife of Shah Jahan, Emperor of the Mughal Empire. It seems to be a marble embroidery and fascinates every tourist who has the incredible opportunity of arriving in front of the Taj Mahal. The architecture is reminscent of the Mughal period, but you can also notice influences of the Persian architectural style.

Other Attractions in Asia:

Asia is home to many other fabulous attractions that have never disappointed their visitors. Here are some more attractions that deserve your attention:

Angkor Wat Temple, Cambodia

Beaches of Bali

Bangkok, Thailand

Golden Triangle, India

Hong Kong, China

Kyoto and Tokyo, Japan

Maldives

Phuket, Thailand

Singapore

Terracotta Warriors, China

What Documents Do You Need to Have When Traveling to Asia?

The number and type of documents you are going to need for your trips to Asia depend on the country you're planning to visit. Here are some details regarding the most important documents tourists need to have on them when visiting the countries of Asia.

Countries That Require a Tourist Visa

Afghanistan

Your visa for Afghanistan must be obtained from an embassy of the Islamic Republic of Afghanistan, and your passport should be valid for at least 6 months from your entry to Afghanistan. You may be denied entry into Afghanistan if your passport holds an Israeli visa, an Israeli border stamp or an Egyptian or Jordanian border stamp issued by an office bordering Israel. Yellow fever vaccination is required if you're arriving from countries with risk of yellow fever transmission.

Bahrain

Tourists must be in possession of a visa when entering Bahrain. Some nationalities are able to buy a tourist visa upon arrival to Bahrain. Keep in mind that payments should be made only by credit card. There is also the possibility to obtain your visa online from Bahrain eVisas. Your passport should be valid for at least 6 months from the date of your arrival to Bahrain.

Bhutan

Tourists arriving to Bhutan must have a valid passport for at least 6 months from their arrival and a visa. Make sure you keep on you copies of these documents. Visas are issued only to tourists that have booked their trip with a local, licensed tour operator or a foreign travel agent. The visa applications will be submitted by the tour operator. Except for Indians, all visitors must obtain visa clearance from Thimphu before their arrival. Visitors (except for Indians) may enter and depart Bhutan only through certain towns: Phuntsoling, Samdrup Jongkhar, and Gelephug (by road) or Paro (by air). For traveling to other districts than Thimphu and Paro you need special permits issued by the Bhutanese Ministry of Home and Cultural Affairs. Travelers arriving from countries with risk of yellow fever transmission will be required to show proof of vaccination.

Burma

People traveling to Burma need to get a visa from the Burmese Embassy or Consulate in their home country and to have a valid passport for at least 6 months from the date they arrive to Burma.

China

The most important document you need to have on you when you visit China, and as a matter of fact all the other Asian countries, is your passport. You should make sure the passport is up-to-date and that it is valid for at least 6 months after your entry to China. You also need a visa that can be obtained at the Chinese Embassy or Consulate-General situated in your country. The tourist visa is also called "L visa." An "L visa" is valid for 3 months prior to travel and 30 days from the moment you enter the Chinese territory.

India

All travelers, except for the citizens of Nepal and Buthan, need a visa for their trip to India. Your visa for India must be obtained before arrival. Depending on the nationality of the applicant, a tourist visa can be issued for a maximum stay of 6 months. If you are planning to stay for less than 72 hours, then you can get a Transit Visa. Traveling by train is the most popular way of transportation in India, so we recommend you book your train tickets in advance for your trip.

Iran

For traveling to Iran you need to obtain a visa from Iran's diplomatic and consular missions. You should make sure you apply for a visa well in advance to your arrival here because it might take some time. Women and girls over the age of 9 should wear a scarf in their visa application. Your passport needs to be valid for at least 6 months from the date you apply for a visa. Proof of yellow fever vaccination is required for people traveling from countries with risk of yellow fever transmission.

Iraq

Tourists who plan to visit Iraq need to obtain a visa from Iraqi embassies or missions. Those traveling to the Kurdistan region will be able to get their tourist visa on arrival. Your passport should be valid for at least 3 months from the date you arrive in Iraq.

Kazakhstan

All visitors need to apply for a visa at the embassy of Kazakhstan in their country. If you don't arrive at one of the 12 international airports of Kazakhstan, you need to register at the OVIR (Office of Visas and Registration). Your passport should be valid for at least 6 months from the day you apply for your visa and should have at least one blank page. Until the end of 2015, foreign citizens are forbidden to travel to Gvardeiskii city, Baikonur city and Karmakshy rayon in the area of Kzylorda, Metebulak in the area of Alma Ata, and on the Kulzhabas railroad in the area of Djambul. Yellow fever vaccination is required for those arriving from countries with risk of yellow fever transmission. You must declare amounts exceeding US$3,000 at border crossings, and you are not allowed to bring prescription medication on this country's territory.

Lebanon

If you want to visit Lebanon, you need to apply for a visa at a Lebanon embassy or diplomatic mission, or at any port of entry into Lebanon. Your visa will be valid for a stay of up to 60 days. When you exit the country, your passport must show a Lebanese entry stamp. Make sure your passport is valid for at least 3 months from your arrival to Lebanon.

Mongolia

Those planning to visit Mongolia need to apply for a visa before their arrival. The tourist visa is valid for 6 months from the issue date and can be used for a stay of up to 30 days in Mongolia. Visitors should have a valid passport for at least 6 months from their arrival to this country. Passengers traveling by train across the China/Mongolia border should expect a delay of a few hours as the railways use different gauges. You are allowed to bring medication into Mongolia only if it's for your own use and you can prove this with prescriptions.

North Korea

You need a visa if you want to visit North Korea. Also, you should register with the Ministry of Foreign Affairs if you visit this country for more than 24 hours. Usually this requirement is fulfilled on your behalf by the hotel you're staying at. Your passport should be valid for the duration of your stay. Proof of yellow fever vaccination is required for travelers arriving from countries with risk of yellow fever transmission.

Pakistan

For your trip to Pakistan, you need a valid passport for at least 6 months after your arrival to the country and a visa that can be obtained at the Pakistani embassy or consulate in your country.

Qatar

You need a visa for visiting Qatar and your passport needs to be valid for at least 6 months from the entry date to Qatar. Depending on nationality, some travelers can obtain their visa on arrival, while others must show a proof of an onward or return ticket, besides their passport and visa. However, it is advisable to apply for a visa before your departure to Qatar. If you can buy your visa upon arrival, you should know that they accept only credit card payments. You may be denied entry into Qatar if your passport holds an Israeli visa, an Israeli border stamp or an Egyptian or Jordanian border stamp issued by an office bordering Israel.

Russia

Tourists who want to visit Russia need to apply for a tourist visa at the Russian embassy in their home country. You should make sure you apply well in advance and check that all the details are entered correctly. For stays longer than 7 days, you need to register with the Federal Migration Service. This requirement is fulfilled automatically by the hotel or the owner of the private property you're staying at. Your passport should be valid for at least 6 months after the expiration date of your visa. All foreign travelers need to sign a migration card made of two parts: one part stays with you and one part will be retained by the Immigration Officer at arrival.

If you travel by train on routes such as Warsaw-Moscow or St Petersburg-Kiev you need to get a transit visa for Belarus before traveling. There are also some rules regarding the amount of money you can import and export (up to 10,000 US dollars–or equivalent–to import and up to 3,000 US dollars to export from Russia without declaring it). If you import over 10,000 US dollars or certain categories of goods like electrical items, jewelry, antiques, and other valuable items, you must complete a customs declaration form. If you complete a declaration, make sure the form is stamped by a Customs official at your port of entry, otherwise your foreign currency and non-declared items may be confiscated when you leave Russia and you may be fined.

Saudi Arabia

All visitors need a visa to enter Saudi Arabia. You can obtain your visa from agencies of Royal Embassy of Saudi Arabia. Your passport should be valid for at least 6 months from the moment of your arrival in Saudi Arabia. You may be refused entry to this country if you were born in Israel or if you've traveled to Israel. Female visitors must be met by their sponsor on arrival.

Sri Lanka

Although it is possible to get your visa for Sri Lanka on your arrival, it is recommended to apply for a visa prior to your trip. You can get a short stay visa (for stays up to 30 days) online at Electronic Travel Authority. Your passport should be valid for a minimum period of 6 months from your arrival to Sri Lanka. You also need to have an onward or return ticket.

Syria

If you want to travel to Syria you need a visa. Those planning to stay here for more than 15 days need to have their visa extended at the immigration office. Your passport should be valid for at least 3 months from the date of your arrival to Syria. If you have an Israeli stamp on your passport, you will probably be denied your entrance. Yellow fever vaccination is required for travelers arriving from countries with risk of yellow fever transmission.

Tajikistan

Tourists need to obtain a tourist visa prior to their arrival in the country. Tourist visas can be obtained from the Tajik embassies in their home country. A tourist visa is valid for up to 60 days. Travelers should also have a valid passport for at least 6 months from the moment they apply for a visa. The passport must have at least two blank pages.

Turkmenistan

Those who plan to visit Turkmenistan should know that they need to apply for a tourist visa at the Turkmen embassy in their country. Their visa will be issued about 20 days after their application. For a fee, they can obtain the visa in 24 hours. They will also need a private or company letter of invitation (for tourists this letter can be issued by a local travel agency). On arrival, you must complete a migration card and pay a migration fee. The card will remain with the authorities. Your passport should be valid for the entire period of your stay in Turkmenistan.

If you are staying for more than 3 days in Turkmenistan, you should register with the State Service of Turkmenistan for the Registration of Foreign Nationals. Those who want to transit Turkmenistan by train need to have a visa. You can be registered at entry and exit points if your stay is not longer than five days and you have a valid transit visa. You won't be able to change your transit visa in-country, and you must notify the authorities if you intend to vary your route through the country.

Uzbekistan

If you're visiting Uzbekistan as a tourist you need to get your visa prior to your arrival. Those who are visiting friends or family also need a letter of invitation. Your passport should be valid for the duration of your stay.

When traveling by rail and crossing into neighboring countries, you should make sure you have an appropriate multi-entry visa for Uzbekistan and the other required visas for the countries you're crossing. You will need special permits for traveling to certain parts of Surxondaryo Province.

Vietnam

Although there is the possibility to get your visa on arrival if you discuss this aspect with legitimate companies that deal with such aspects, it is safer to get your tourist visa from the Vietnamese embassy in your area. Your passport should be valid for at least 1 month from the date your Vietnam visa will expire. If arriving from countries with risk of yellow fever transmission, a yellow fever vaccination proof is required.

Yemen

Those traveling to Yemen need to apply for a visa prior to their arrival here. Their passport should be valid at least for the duration of their stay. People traveling from countries with a risk of yellow fever vaccination transmission should have proof of their vaccination.

Countries Where You Can Get Your Visa on Arrival

Bangladesh

If you want to obtain a visa for Bangladesh you need to have a valid passport (and proof of yellow fever vaccination if you're arriving from countries with risk of yellow fever transmission). However, it is recommended to obtain your visa prior to your arrival to Bangladesh and also not to travel in the area of Chittagong Hill Tracts, due to local violence and kidnapping.

Cambodia

Tourist visas can be obtained at your arrival at the airports Phnom Penh and Siem Reap, or at certain land borders. If you want, you can obtain your visa at the Cambodian embassy in your country, prior to your arrival here. Your tourist visa is valid for 30 days from the day you enter

Cambodian territory and can be extended once for another 30 day period. You should have a passport valid for at least 6 months from the date of your entry. Proof of yellow fever vaccination is required if traveling from countries with risk of yellow fever transmission. You should also have proof of an onward or return ticket. You have to pay a departure fee when flying from one of the two airports mentioned above.

Indonesia

You will obtain your tourist visa on arrival if you have a valid passport and onward or return tickets. The tourist visa is valid for a stay of up to 30 days.

Jordan

Your visa for Jordan can be obtained at your arrival at any port of entry to Jordan, except the King Hussein Bridge at the Jordan/Israel border. This visa will be valid for 1 month. Your visa can be extended once for a stay of up to 6 months. If you want to get to Israel and the Palestinian Authority, you should get a multiple entry visa. Your passport should be valid for a period of 6 months from your arrival to Jordan. Yellow fever vaccination is required for travelers arriving from countries with risk of yellow fever transmission.

Kuwait

Tourists can get a free 30-day entry permit at their arrival in Kuwait. They should have a valid passport for a period of at least 6 months from the entry data. There are cases when travelers who have an Israeli stamp on their passports aren't allowed to enter Kuwait.

Laos

Visa conditions in Laos change regularly, so you should make sure you get in touch with the Laos embassy before your trip. Currently, you can obtain a visa on arrival, for a fee. Make sure you get your passport stamp because otherwise you can be arrested and ordered to pay a large fine. Your passport should be valid for at least 6 months from the moment you enter Laos. Proof of yellow fever vaccination is required for passengers traveling from countries with risk of yellow fever transmission. You need to get permission to travel to certain regions of Vientiane and Xieng Khoung provinces.

Maldives

Tourist visas are issued upon arrival and are valid for a period of 30 days. Visas can be extended for a total stay of 90 days. You need to have proof of an onward or return ticket. Your passport should be valid for the duration of your stay in Maldives. If you want to visit non-resort islands you need to get express permission from the Maldivian authorities. Yellow fever vaccination is mandatory for travelers arriving from countries with risk of yellow fever transmission.

Nepal

You can get your visa on arrival at the Kathmandu airport or apply for a visa at the Nepal embassy in your country. Your visa will be valid for up to 60 days from your arrival. Make sure you have a passport valid for at least the duration of your stay in Nepal. If you're planning to visit Tibet, an autonomous region of China, you must book an organized tour group. Permits are issued by the Chinese embassy in Kathmandu.

Oman

You can get a visa on arrival to Oman at any land, sea, or air entry port. You can extend your visa for up to 1 month. Your passport should be valid for at least 6 months from the date of your entry to Oman. If you have prescription drugs on you, make sure they are accompanied by a copy of your prescription.

United Arab Emirates

You can obtain your visa on arrival (for a stay of up to 30 days) as long as you have a valid passport for at least 6 months from the date of your arrival. However, there are some countries that do not benefit from this privilege and their citizens must obtain a visa prior to their arrival. A tourist visa can be obtained online and is valid for 30 days.

Countries That Don't Require a Tourist Visa

Brunei

Travelers don't need a visa to visit Brunei if they plan to stay here for up to 90 days (the period may differ depending on the nationality). You should make sure your entry stamp mentions the validity of your stay. You need to have a valid passport for at least 6 months from your arrival to Brunei. You will need to pay a small departure fee.

Hong Kong

Although Hong Kong is now part of China, it stays a Special Administrative Region, so tourists will be able to visit this place without having to apply for a visa. The visa-free period depends on the nationality of each visitor. UK citizens can stay in Hong Kong for up to 6 months before applying for a visa, while American and

Canadian citizens benefit from a 3 month stay. The passport should be valid for the duration of your stay. If you're planning to get to China from Hong Kong you need to obtain a Chinese visa.

Israel

Tourists don't need a visa to visit Israel for a period of up to 3 months. On entry, visitors will be given an entry card instead of an entry stamp on their passports. This card is evidence of legal entry into Israel and may be required at any crossing points into the Occupied Palestinian Territories, so it is wise to keep it on them until they leave Israeli territory. Tourists should also have a passport on them, valid for at least 6 months from their entry into Israel and the Occupied Palestinian Territories.

Video cameras, laptops, and other similar items must be declared at the Israeli authorities. Carrying a laptop in the passenger cabin might be prohibited, usually these types of items are sent separately to their destination. Some travelers arriving at the Allenby Bridge crossing with Jordan or Ben Gurion Airport have reported to having had their passport stamped "Palestinian Authority only" or "Judea and Samaria only." These stamps limit travelers to West Bank destinations only and don't allow them to enter Israel or Jerusalem. There are also reports that confirm the fact that certain visitors had to sign a form that prohibited them from visiting Israel and Jerusalem, limiting their visits to West Bank destinations.

Japan

A tourist visa is not required for your visit to Japan as long as your stay is not longer than 90 days. You might need to present your onward or return ticket. Make sure your passport is valid for your entire stay in Japan.

Kyrgyzstan

Citizens of countries such as USA, UK, Canada, Germany, Italy, Spain, etc. don't need a visa for visiting Kyrgyzstan. They can stay on this country's territory for up to 60 days without having to apply for a visa. However, there are countries that don't enjoy this privilege, so their citizens should apply for a visa before their arrival here. Their visa will be valid for up to 90 days. All visitors should have a passport on them valid for at least 3 months from the date of their arrival to Kyrgyzstan.

Malaysia

You don't need a visa to visit Malaysia as long as your stay is not longer than 3 months. Your passport should be valid for at least 6 months from the date of your arrival to this country.

Philippines

Tourists don't need a visa if they spend less than 30 days in the Philippines. For longer stays (up to 59 days) you can get a tourist visa from the Philippines Embassy in your home country. You need to have a valid passport on you (make sure it is valid for the following 6 months after your arrival), onward or return ticket, and, in some cases, proof of yellow fever vaccination.

Singapore

For stays up to 30 to 90 days in Singapore (depending on the nationality), visitors don't need a visa. They do need, however, a valid passport for at least 6 months after their departure from this country. You should also have an onward or return ticket on you and you may be asked to show proof of sufficient funds for your stay.

Importing certain controlled drugs and pirated copyright material is prohibited and there are restrictions on entering with items like replica guns, radio communications equipment, and weapons and ammunition (including empty cartridge cases and air guns). You should know that certain medicines can be considered controlled substances in Singapore, so it is recommended to apply for prior authorization if you want to bring medicine to Singapore. Yellow fever vaccination is required for travelers arriving from countries with risk of yellow fever transmission.

South Korea

Tourists can visit South Korea for up to 90 days without a visa. They must have a passport on them, valid for at least 3 months from the date of their entry to South Korea and an onward or return ticket.

Taiwan

There is no need for tourist visa during your trip to Taiwan as long as your trip is not longer than 90 days. This privilege might be extended once for another period of 90 days. If you're planning for a longer stay, you have to apply for a tourist visa before your arrival to Taiwan. Your passport should be valid for at least 6 months after you enter Taiwan.

Thailand

For stays of up to 30 days there is no need for a tourist visa. However, there are some cases, depending on the origin country, when tourists need to get a visa on arrival and to show proof of an onward or return ticket. Either way, you need to have a passport on you, valid for 6 months after your entry to Thailand.

Once-in-a-Lifetime Trainride Experiences

If you want to enjoy luxurious train journeys that will take you back in time, when aristocrats traveled around the world by train, enjoying the utmost comfort and impeccable services, or simply unique train trips, you should book a seat with one of these trains:

Eastern & Oriental Express

Probably the most elegant train in Asia, the Eastern & Oriental Express will carry you to the magical lands of Thailand, Singapore, Malaysia, and Laos. Expect the most luxurious interior setting and you will still be taken by surprise by the splendor of this train's suites and cabins. The train also has elegant lounges with panoramic windows and 5-star restaurants that serve Eastern and European cuisine. Breakfast will be served in the comfort of your own suite or cabin. The prices vary depending on the journey you select, but let's just say that you need to feel a bit aristocratic to afford an Eastern & Oriental Express journey (the prices start at $2000/person).

The Maharajas Express

A luxurious train that will carry you through the mystic land of India, the Maharajas Express will bring you back to the 19th century, when opulence was a must for every rich traveler. Each cabin enjoys an elegant setting and all the modern facilities you need for a comfortable vacation. We just love that every suite has panoramic windows from where India can be admired. The train has 2 restaurants decorated with period furniture and a total capacity of 82 passengers. Depending on the chosen itinerary and the type of suite, passengers will have to pay from $3,850/suite.

Royal Rajasthan on Wheels

A colorful train, dressed in expensive fabrics and decorated with furniture worthy of a Maharaja, the Royal Rajasthan on Wheels offers a spectacular journey through the "Land of Maharajas," Rajasthan. The itinerary includes 8 days spent on a fabulous train that will offer you an unforgettable train journey that begins and ends in Delhi. The 41 suites enjoy panoramic windows, wood furniture, silk and velvet fabrics, and wall-to-wall carpeting. All suites are equipped with modern facilities and offer wireless internet. The 2 restaurants welcome guests with Rajasthani, Indian, Continental, and Chinese specialties. The train also has an SPA center, for travelers to be pampered. The prices start from $4,000/person.

Golden Eagle

Truly a hotel on wheels, Golden Eagle will carry you to discover the sceneries of

Russia, Mongolia, China, Kazakhstan, Uzbekistan, and many other places that will fascinate and amaze. There are many itineraries for you to choose from, but you should make sure you reserve 2 weeks for a journey with the Golden Eagle. Like all the other trains we've mentioned here, this train too enjoys panoramic windows and opulent suites equipped with luxurious furniture and facilities. The prices start at $15,000 and include both accommodations on board the train and in hotels, meals, drinks, transfers, tours, etc.

Deccan Odyssey

The Deccan Odyssey is a modern but elegant train that will carry you through the State of Maharashtra. The train is decorated with contemporary furniture, offering a luxurious setting to each traveler, regardless of the type of cabin chosen. It has 21 carriages, restaurants, lounge and conference cars, and a capacity of 80 passengers. The train is equipped with an SPA center and offers internet access. A journey with the Deccan Odyssey starts and ends in Mumbai and is a great opportunity to admire unearthly sceneries.

Palace on Wheels

A 14-coach train, the Palace on Wheels is one of the most famous trains in India. The carriages remind you of the saloons of Maharajas, so you will get a chance to actually experience the lifestyle of a royal. The train's restaurant serves international cuisine, and the lounge is ideal for just hanging out with your friends and admiring the incredible, beautiful sceneries India has to offer. You can also find an SPA car. Your trip will start and end in Delhi. The prices of an 8-day itinerary start from $3,640/person and include accommodation, full catering, beverages, entrance to touristic attractions, cultural performances, a camel ride at Sam Sand Dunes (Jaisalmer), a boat ride at Lake Pichola (Udaipur), and a rickshaw ride at Bharatpur.

Imperial Russia

If we're talking about Russia, we're definitely talking about opulence and unseen luxury. This train brings together absolutely fabulous pieces of furniture and last-generation facilities. All the suites are VIP. It has 2 restaurant cars and a bar. The train will follow the Trans-Siberian Railway and your journey will start in St. Petersburg and end in Irkutsk. There is also the option for booking the itinerary that includes Beijing as final destination. The prices start at €8,500/person.

Train Stations in Bangladesh

Abdulpur Train station
Natore District

Ahsanganj Train Station
Naogaon District

Akkelpur Train Station
Akkelpur, Joypurhat District

Bagerhat Train Station
Old Rupsa Bagerhat Rd, Bagerhat

Bagjana Train Station
Joypurhat District

Banani Train Station
Dhaka-Mymensingh Hwy, Dhaka, Dhaka
Division

Bhairab Bazar Train Station

Bhairab Bazar, Dhaka Division, Bangladesh

Biman Bandar (Airport) Train Station
Mymensingh Hwy, Dhaka District, 1230, Bangladesh
Phone: 8924239

Biral Train Station
Dinajpur District

Bogra Train Station
College Rd, Bogra 5800, Bangladesh

Burimari Train Station
Lalmonirhat District

Chilahati Train Station
Nilphamari District

Chittagong Train Station
Chittagong

Darshana Train Station

Damurhuda Upazila, Chuadanga District

Dhaka Cantonment Train Station

Tongi Diversion Rd, Dhaka, Bangladesh

Faridpur Train Station

Station Rd, Faridpur, Bangladesh
Phone: 635162, Station Manager-01711-
691550

Feni Junction Train Station

Feni Railway Station Rd, Feni, Bangladesh

Gouripur Train Station

Gouripur, Dhaka Division, Bangladesh

Hili Train Station

Hakimpur, Dinajpur District

Iswardi Train station

Pabna District

Jafarpur Train Station

Joypurhat District

Jamalganj Train Station
Joypurhat District

Jamtoil Train Station
Lablu Talukder Road, Sirajganj, Rajshahi Division, Bangladesh

Jessore Train Station
7400 Jessore, Khulna
Phone: + 880421-65019 /+880421-67995

Joydebpur Train Station
Gazipur District

Joypurhat Train Station
Joypurhat District

Kamalapur Train Station
Kamlapur, Dhaka District

Khulna Junction Train Station

Railway Rd, Khulna, Bangladesh

Kulaura Junction Train Station

Rajnagar - Kulaura Rd, Kulaura, Bangladesh

Phone: 9358634, 8315857, 9331822, 01711691612

Laksham Train Station

Daulatganj, Exit Rd, Laksam, Bangladesh

Lalmonirhat Train Station

Lalmonirhat District

Mogalhat Train Station

Lalmonirhat District

Panchbibi Train Station

Joypurhat District

Parbatipur Train Station

Dinajpur District

Puranapail Train Station
Joypurhat District
Phone: 776040

Rajshahi Train Station
Rajshahi District

Rohanpur Train Station
Nawabganj District

Santahar Train Station
Santahar Rd, Santahar Pouroshova, Bogra District

Sirajganj Train Station
Sirajganj, Rajshahi, Bangladesh

Syedpur Train Station
Railway Rd, Saidpur, Bangladesh

Sylhet Train Station
Train Station Way, Sylhet Division

Phone : 717036 Station Manager-01711-691656

Tangail Train Station
Station Rd, Tangail, Bangladesh

Tejgaon Train Station
Station Rd, Dhaka, Dhaka Division, Bangladesh

Tilakpur Train Station
Joypurhat District

Zia Airport Train Station
Dhaka - Mymensingh Hwy, Dhaka 1230, Bangladesh

Train Stations in Burma
Mandalay

Amarapura Butar Train Station
Bu Tar St, Aramapura District, Mandalay

Aung Pin Le Train Station
Chanmyathazi, Mandalay, Mandalay Division

Be Lin Train Station
Be Lin, Myanmar

Han Za Train Station
Hanzar, Myanmar

Khin Ban Train Station
Khin Ban, Myanmar

Ku Me Lan Train Station
Ku Me Lan, Myanmar

Mandalay Train Station

78th St and 30th St Junction Chanayethazan, Mandalay, Mandalay Division

Minsu Train Station

Minsu, Myanmar

Myitnge Train Station

Myitnge, Amarapura, Mandalay Region 05

Myittha Train Station

2, Myittha, Myanmar

Myo Haung Train Station

Myo Haung, Myanmar

Myohaung Train Station

Myohaung, Myanmar

Nwa Do Train Station

Nwa Do, Myanmar

Nyaung Yan Train Station

Nyaungyan, Myanmar

Odokkon Train Station

Odokkon, Myanmar

Paleik Train Station

Paleik, Myanmar

Sa Mun Train Station

Sa Mun, Myanmar

Sagaing Train Station

Sagaing, Myanmar

Shanzu Train Station

Shanzu, Myanmar

Shwe Kyet Yet Train Station

Shwe Kyet Yet, Myanmar

Sintgaing Train Station

Sintgaing, Myanmar

Ta Gun Daing Train Station
Ta Gun Daing, Myanmar

Tada-U Train Station
Tada-U, Kyaukse, Myanmar

Tha Pyay Taung Train Station
Thabyedaung, Myanmar

Thazi Train Station
Thazi, Myanmar

The Daw Train Station
Thea Taw, Myanmar

Ya Ta Na Gu Train Station
Ya Ta Na Gu, Myanmar

Ywa Htaung Train Station
Ywa Htaung Bu Tar St, Sagaing, Myanmar

Ywa Pale Train Station

Ywa Pale, Myanmar

Taungoo

Ela Train Station

Aye Lar, Myanmar

Hnge Taik Train Station

Hnge Taik, Myanmar

Htein-In Train Station

Htein-In, Myanmar

In Gyin Kan Train Station

In Gyin Kan, Myanmar

Inn Gon Train Station

Inn Gon, Myanmar

Kay Tu Ma Ti Train Station

Kay Tu Ma Ti, Myanmar

Kone Gyi Train Station
Kone Gyi, Myanmar

Kyee Taw Train Station
Kyee Taw, Myanmar

Kyidaunggan Train Station
Kyidaunggan, Myanmar

Kyun Kone Train Station
Asian Highway 1, Kyungon, Kyun Kone, Myanmar

Ma Gyi Bin Train Station
Ma Gyi Bin, Myanmar

Myo Hla Train Station
Asian Highway 1, Myo Hla

Nay Pyi Taw Train Station
Naypyidaw Union Territory, Myanmar

Nyaung Lunt Train Station

Nyaung Lunt, Myanmar

Pyawbwe Train Station
Asian Highway 1, Pyawbwe, Myanmar

Pyi Win Train Station
Pyi Win, Myanmar

Pyinmana Train Station
Pyinmana, Myanmar

Pyok Kwe Train Station
Pyok Kwe, Myanmar

Shan Ywa Train Station
Shan Ywa, Myanmar

Shwe Da Train Station
Shwe Da, Myanmar

Shwe Myo Train Station
Shwe Myo, Myanmar

Sin Byu Gyun Train Station
Sin Byu Gyun, Myanmar

Sin The Train Station
Sin The, Myanmar

Swar Train Station
Asian Highway 1, Swar, Myanmar

Taungoo Train Station
Taungoo, Myanmar

Tha Wat Ti Train Station
Thar Wut Hti, Myanmar

Tha Yet Kone Train Station
Tha Yet Kone, Myanmar

Thar Ga Ya Train Station
Thar Ga Ya, Myanmar

Tut Kone Train Station
Tatkon, Myanmar

Yae Ni Train Station
Asian Highway 1, Yae Ni

Yamethin Train Station
Thi La Wa St, Yamethin, Myanmar

Yedashe Train Station
Yedashe, Myanmar

Ywadaw Train Station
Ywadaw, Myanmar

Yangon

Aung Thu Kha Train Station
Kyaik Khauk Pagoda Rd, Thanlyin

Bant Bway Kone Train Station
Bant Bway Kone, Myanmar

Dagon University Train Station

Yangon, Myanmar

Daik-U Train Station
Bu Tar St, Daik-U, Myanmar

Ein Chay Lay Se Train Station
Ein Chay Lay Se, Myanmar

Hpaung Taw Thi Train Station
Zay St, Hpaung Taw Thi, Myanmar

Htongyi Train Station
Htongyi, Myanmar

Industrial Zone Train Station
Yangon, Myanmar

Ka Nyut Kwin Train Station
Asian Highway 1, Ka Nyut Kwin, Myanmar

Ka Toke Train Station
Kannyinaung St, Ka Toke, Myanmar

Kawt Che Train Station
Kawt Che, Myanmar

Kyaikzagaw Train Station
Kyaik Sa Kaw, Myanmar

Kyauk Tan Train Station
Main road, Kyauk Tan, Myanmar

Kyauktaga Train Station
Asian Highway 1, Kyauktaga, Myanmar

Kywe Pwe Train Station
Kywe Pwe, Myanmar

Ngahtetgyi Train Station
Yangon - Mandalay Hwy, Ngahtetgyi, Myanmar

Nyaung Chay Htauk Train Station
Asian Highway 1, Nyaung Chay Htauk, Myanmar

Nyaung Le Bin Train Station

Western Market Rd, Nyaung Lay Pin, Myanmar

Nyaung Pin Thar Train Station

Asian Highway 1, Nyaung Pin Thar, Myanmar

Oak Po Su Train Station

Yangon, Myanmar

Oke Twin Train Station

Asian Highway 1, Oktwin, Myanmar

Payagyi Train Station

Hpa Yar Gyi, Myanmar

Payathonzu Train Station

Payathonzu, Myanmar

Pe Nwe Kone Train Station

Penwegon, Myanmar

Pegu (Bago) Train Station
Bago, Myanmar

Pein Za Loke Train Station
Pein Za Loke, Myanmar

Phayagale Train Station
Hpa Yar Ka Lay, Myanmar

Phyu Train Station
Asian Highway 1, Phyu, Myanmar

Pyin Pone Train Station
Pyinbongyi, Bago, Myanmar

Pyuntaza Train Station
Yangon - Mandalay Hwy, Pyuntasa, Myanmar

Shwe Hlay Train Station
Shwe Hlay, Bago, Myanmar

Shwe Hle Train Station

Bago, Myanmar

Shwe Tan Train Station

Shwe Tan, Myanmar

Tar Wa Train Station

Tawa, Bago, Myanmar

Taw Kywel Inn Train Station

Asian Highway 1, Taw Kywel Inn

Taw Wi Train Station

Asian Highway 1, Taw Wi, Myanmar

Thaung Taing Kone Train Station

Thaung Taing Kone, Myanmar

Thu Htay Kone Train Station

Thu Htay Kone , Myanmar

Wan Be Inn Train Station

Wan Be Inn, Myanmar

Yin Taik Kone Train Station
Yin Taik Kone, Kyauktaga, Myanmar

Zay Ya Wa Di Train Station
Asian Highway 1, Zay Ya Wa Di, Myanmar

Yangon (Central)

Yangon Circular Rail Line

Ahlone Train Station
Ahlon Rd, Yangon

Aung San Train Station
Mingaladon Township, Yangon

Bauk Htaw Train Station
Yankin, Yangon

Da Nyin Gon Train Station

Khayae Pin Rd, Yangon

Gaw Gwin (Golf Course) Train Station
Khayae Pin Rd, Yangon

Gyo Gone Train Station
Baho Rd, Yangon

Han Thar Waddy Train Station
Hanthawaddy Rd, Yangon

Hledan Train Station
Kyun Chan 1 St, Yangon

Insein Train Station
Insein, Yangon

Kamaryut Train Station
Baho Rd, Yangon

Kan Be Train Station
Wai Za Yan Tar Rd, Yangon

Kyaik Ka Le Train Station
Yangon - Mandalay Hwy, Yangon

Kyauk Yae Twin Train Station
North Okkalapa, Yangon

Kyeemyindaing Train Station
Upper Kyi Myin Daing Rd, Yangon

Lanmadaw Train Station
Myoma Kyaung St, Latha, Yangon

Mah Lwa Gone Train Station
Myo Pat St, Tamwe, Yangon

Mingalardon Market Train Station
Mingaladon Township, Yangon

Mingalardon Train Station
Mingaladon Township, Yangon

Myittar Nyunt Train Station
Dagon Lwin St, Tamwe, Yangon

Oke Kyin Train Station
Oke Kyin Bu Tar Yon St, Okkyin, Yangon

Okkalarpa Train Station
North Okkalapa, Yangon

Pa Ywet Seik Kone Train Station
North Okkalapa, Yangon

Pan Hlaing Train Station
Pann Hlaing St, Yangon

Parami Train Station
South Okkalapa, Yangon

Phawt Kan Train Station
Insein, Yangon

Phaya Lan Train Station
Shwedagon Pagoda Rd, Yangon

Puzundaung Train Station

Mingalar Taung Nyunt, Yangon

Pyay Lan Train Station

Pyay Rd, Yangon

Shan Lan Train Station

Baho Rd, Yangon

Tadalay Train Station

North Okkalapa, Yangon

Tamwe Train Station

Tamwe, Yangon

Tha Mine Train Station

Baho Rd, Yangon

Thiri Myaing Train Station

Baho Rd, Hlaing, Yangon

Wai Bar Gi Train Station

Mingaladon Township, Yangon

Yaegu Train Station
Mya Sabai St, Mayangone, Yangon

Yangon Train Station
Kun Chan Rd, Kyauktada Township, Yangon
Phone: 274027, 202175, 202176, 202178

Ywa Ma Train Station
Insein, Yangon

Yangon-Mandalay Line

Dar Pein Train Station
Dar Pein, Myanmar

Hnin Si Gone Train Station
Thingangyun, Yangon

Lay Daung Kan Train Station
No 2 Rd, Ledaunggan, Myanmar

Nga Moe Yeik Train Station
Thingangyun, Yangon

Thin Gan Gyun Train Station
Thingangyun, Yangon

Toe Kyaung Ka Lay Train Station
No 2 Rd, Yangon

Ywar Thar Gyi Train Station
Ywar Thar Gyi Township, Yangon

Train Stations in Cambodia

Phnom Penh Royal Train Station
Sangkat Sras Chak, Daun Penh District,
Phnom Penh
Phone: 023 992 379

Pursat Train Station
National Highway 5, Krong Pursat

Battambang Train Station
Preah Vihea St, Krong Battambang

Poipet Train Station
5, Poi Pet, Krong Paoy Paet

Takéo Train Station
Takéo, Krong Doun Kaev

Kampot Train Station
Kampot, Cambodia

Sihanoukville Train Station

Sihanoukville, Krong Preah Sihanouk, Cambodia

Train Stations in China

Train stations in Anhui Province

Train stations in Anqing Municipality

Anqing Train Station

No.192, Yingbin Road, Anqing

Phone: 0556-5027222

Anqing West Train Station

Huaining County, Anhui Province

Tongcheng Train Station

Tongzong Road, Tongcheng City, Anhui

Susong Train Station

Susong County, Anhui

Taihu Train Station

No.215, Gaojie Road, Taihu County, Anhui

Tianzhushan Train Station

No.646, Wanguo Road, Meicheng Town, Qianshan County, Anhui

Train stations in Bengbu Municipality

Bengbu Train Station
No.638, Huaihe Road, Bengbu
Phone: 0552-3922222

Guzhen Train Station
Huihe Road(West Section), Chengguan Town, Guzhen County, Bengbu

Train stations in Bozhou Municipality

Bozhou Train Station
Zhanqian Road, Bozhou
Phone: 0558－5327642

Guoyang Train Station
Zhanqian Road, New Town Community, Chengguan Town, Guoyang County, Anhui
Phone: 0561-2125641

Train stations in Chizhou Municipality

Chizhou Train Station
Zhanqian Zone, Chizhou, Anhui
Phone: 0566-3213366

Dongzhi Train Station
Jiangfanzu, Maotian Village, Yaodu Town,
Dongzhi County, Anhui

Train stations in Chuzhou Municipality

Chuzhou Train Station
No.295, Tianchang Road, Langya District,
Chuzhou
Phone: 0550-2114222

Mingguang Train Station
No.46, Chezhan Road, Mingguang City,
Chuzhou

Quanjiao Train Station

Rulin Avenue, Quanjiao County, Anhui

Fengyang Train Station
Chezhan Street, Fengyang County, Chuzhou

Luqiao Train Station
Yexi Street Block, Luqiao Town, Dingyuan County, Chuzhou
Phone: 0550-4300346

Train stations in Fuyang Municipality

Fuyang Train Station
No.1, Shuguang Road, Fuyang
Phone:0558-2483222

Funan Train Station
Phone: 0558-2487252

Yingshang Train Station
Huangqiao Town, Yingshang County, Fuyang

Phone: 0558-2487302

Train stations in Hefei Municipality

Hefei Train Station
No.1, Zhanqian Road, Yaohai District, Hefei
Phone: 0551-4243311

Hefei West Train Station
No.400, Wangjiang West Road, Shushan District, Hefei, Anhui

Feidong Train Station
Zhanbei Road, Feidong County, Anhui

Lujiang Train Station
Wanshan Town, Lujiang County, Anhui

Feixi Train Station
Zhanqian Road, Shangpai Town, Feixi County, Anhui

Chaobei Train Station
Langanji Town, Juchao District, Chaohu, Anhui

Shuijiahu Train Station
Changhuai Road, Changfeng County, Hefei
Phone: 0551-2715483

Ketan Train Station
Ketan Town, Lujiang County, Anhui

Train stations in Huainan Municipality

Huainan Train Station
No.131, Shungeng Middle Road, Tianjia'an District, Huainan
Phone: 0554-2113222

Zhangji Train Station
Dazhuang Village, Zhangji Town, Fengtai County, Huainan
Phone: 0554-2317292

Train stations in Huaibei Municipality

Huaibei Train Station

Zhahe Road, Xiangshan District, Huaibei, Anhui

Phone: 0561-2122222

Qinglongshan Train Station

Qinglong Mountain Town, Lieshan District, Huaibei, Anhui

Phone: 0561-2123202

Train stations in Huangshan Municipality

Huangshan Train Station

No.4, Zhanqian Road, Tunxi District, Huangshan Municipality, Anhui

Phone: 0559-2116222

Shexian Train Station

No.89, Xin'an Road, Shexian, Anhui

Qimen Train Station

Rd. 10, Train Station of Qishan Town, Qimen County, Anhui

Train stations in Lu'an Municipality

Lu'an Train Station

No.7, Jiefang South Road, Yu'an District, Lu'an, Anhui

Jinzhai Train Station

Jinzhai County, Anhui

Yeji Train Station

Reform Experimental Development Zone, Yeji, Lu'an, Anhui

Phone: 0564-2722114

Shucheng Train Station

No.38, Dongsheng Road, Sub-District of Hangbu Town, Shucheng County, Lu'an, Anhui

Train stations in Ma'anshan Municipality

Ma'anshan Train Station

No.103, Hongqi North Road, Huashan District, Ma'anshan, Anhui

Train stations in Tongling Municipality

Tongling East Train Station

Tongling Municipality Municipality, Anhui Province

Phone: 0562-2124004

Train stations in Suzhou Municipality

Suzhou Train Station

Gongren Road, Yongqiao District, Suzhou, Anhui

Phone: 0557-2120242

Dangshan Train Station

Dangshan County, Anhui Province

Phone: 0557-2251332

Huangkou Train Station

Huangkou Town, Xiaoxian, Anhui

Phone: 0557-2213962

Train stations in Wuhu Municipality

Wuhu Train Station

No.1, Beijing East Road, Jinghu District, Wuhu Municipality, Anhui

Phone: 0553-2822222

Yuxikou Train Station

Jiujiang District, Wuhu Municipality Municipality, Anhui

Train stations in Xuancheng Municipality

Xuancheng Train Station

No.110, Diezhang East Road, Xuanzhou City, Anhui

Phone: 0563-2112161

Guangde Train Station
No.1, Hengshan North Road, Guangde County, Anhui

Ningguo Train Station
No.101, Yingbin Road, Ningguo City, Anhui

Jixi Train Station
Yangzhi South Road, Jixi County, Anhui
Phone: 0563-2313662

Train Stations in Anshun Province

Anshun Train Station
Xixiu District, Anshun Municipality
Phone: 028-12306

Train Stations in Baoding Province

Baoding Train Station

No.118, Xinhua Road, Baoding, Hebei

Laiyuan Train Station
Laiyuan Train Station, Laiyuan County, Hebei

Gaobeidian Train Station
Train Station of Gaobeidian City, Hebei

Dingzhou Train Station
No.62, Bolingbei, Dingzhou City, Hebei

Xushui Train Station
No.12, Chezhan Street, Kangming Middle Road, Xushui County, Baoding, Hebei

Wangdu Train Station
No.8, Zhonghua Street, Wangdu County, Baoding, Hebei

Zhuozhou Train Station
No.73, Yingbin Road, Zhuozhou City, Hebei

Baijian Train Station
Zhaogezhuang Town, Laishui County, Hebei

Nanchengsi Train Station
Nanchengsi Train Station, Nanchengsi Township, Yixian, Hebei

Train Stations in Beijing Province

Anding Train Station
Anding Town, Daxing District

Badaling Train Station
216 Provincial Rd, Yanqing County

Beijing (Central) Train Station
No. 13 A, Maojiawan Hutong, Dongcheng District
Phone: 010-51019999

Beijing South Train Station

Yongdingmenwai Dajie, Chongwen District
Phone: 51867999

Beijing West Train Station

No.118, East Lianhuachi Road, Fengtai District, Beijing
Phone: 010-63216253, 010-63216263, 010-63216273

Beijing East Train Station

No.27, Baiziwan Rd, Chaoyang

Beijing North Train Station

No.1, North Binhe Road, Xicheng District

Beizhai Train Station

Changping Train Station

Xianiantou Village, Machikou, Changping District

Changping North Train Station

North Station, Changping, Changping District

Dahuichang Train Station
Large Lime Works Train Station, Large Lime Works Village, Fengtai District

Daxing Train Station
Chezhan Rd, Daxing

Guangao Train Station
Guangao Village, Nanshao Town, Changping District

Guanting West Train Station

Gushankou Train Station
Xiazhongyuan Village, Hancunhe Town, Fangshan District

Huairou Train Station
No.1, Fuqian East Street, Huai'rou District

Huairou North Train Station
North Station, Huairou, Huai'rou District

Huangcun Train Station
Linxiao Road, Huangcun Town, Daxing District

Kangzhuang Train Station
Zhanbei St, Yanqing, Beijing

Lianggezhuang Train Station
Zhoukoudian Town, Fangshan District

Luopoling Train Station
Wangping Town, Mentougou District

Miaocheng Train Station
Huai'rou Area

Miyun Train Station
No.1, Chezhan Road, Miyun County

Nanguancun Train Station

Nanguan Village, Qinglonghu Town, Fangshan District

Nankou Train Station
No.84, Jiaotong Street, Nankou Town, Changping District

Pingyu Train Station
Shidu Village, Shidu Town, Fangshan District

Qinghe Train Station
Haidian District

Qinghuayuan Train Station
Opposite Beihang Ximen, Dayun Village, Zhichun Road, Haidian District

Sanhezhuang Train Station
Zhangfang Town, Fangshan District

Sanjiadian Train Station

Mentougou District

Shahe Train Station
No.1, Zhanqian Road, Shahe Town, Changping District

Shangwan Train Station
Shangwanzhan, Qinglonghu Town, Fangshan District

Shidu Train Station
Shidu Village, Shidu Town, Fangshan District

Shijingshan South Train Station
No.52, Xiaoguozhuang West Road, Lugouqiao, Fengtai District

Shuangqiao Train Station
N Shuangqiao Rd, Chaoyang

Shunyi Train Station

No.17, Zhanqian North Street, Shunyi District

Weishanzhuang Train Station
Weishanzhuang Town, Daxing Zone, Hebei

Xiehejian Train Station
Miaofengshan, Mentougou District

Yanchi Train Station
Yanchi Town, Mentougou District

Yanhecheng Train Station
Zhaitang Town, Mentougou District

Yanshan Train Station
No.7, Yanshan Middle Road, Fangshan District

Yunjunsi Train Station

Zhangxin Train Station

Zhuwo Train Station

Yanchi Town, Mentougou District

Train Stations in Bijie Prefecture

Caohai Train Station

Weining County, Bijie City, Guizhou

Phone: 028-12306

Train Stations in Cangzhou Province

Cangzhou Train Station

No.2, Xinhua Middle Road, Xinhua District, Cangzhou, Hebei

Changzhou West Train Station

Tou, W. End, Beijing Road, Cangxian, Cangzhou, Hebei

Qingxian Train Station

No.72, Yingbin Road, Qingxian, Cangzhou, Hebei

Dongguang Train Station

Yongxing Road, Dongguang County, Hebei

Botou Train Station

Shengli East Road, Botou City, Hebei

Wuqiao Train Station

Changjiang Road, Wuqiao County, Hebei

Suning Train Station

Zhanqian Street, Suning County, Cangzhou, Hebei

Renqiu Train Station

No.1, Bohai Road, Renqiu City, Hebei

Train Stations in Chongqing

Baisha Train Station

Baisha Town, Jiangjin District

Phone: 028-12306

Beibei Train Station
Longfeng First Village, Beibei District
Phone: 028-12306

Changhebian Train Station
Dazu County
Phone: 028-12306

Changshou Train Station
Yanjia Town, Changshou District
Phone: 028-12306

Chongqing North Train Station
Longtousi, Tiangongdian Subdistrict, Yubei District
Phone: 023-63862707

Chongqing South Train Station
No.222, Tielu Second Village, Jiulongpo District
Phone: 028-12306

Fenggaopu Train Station

Fenggao Town, Rongchang County

Phone: 028-12306

Fenshuisi Train Station

Fenshui Town, Wanzhou District

Phone: 028-12306

Ganshui Train Station

Ganshui Town, Qijiang County

Phone: 028-12306

Guangshunchang Train Station

Guangshunchang Town, Rongchang County

Phone: 028-12306

Hechuan Train Station

Gaoyang Village, Nanjin Subdistrict, Hechuan District

Phone: 028-12306

Jiangjin Train Station
Shangxin Rd, Jiangjin

Liangping Train Station
Hexing Town, Liangping County
Phone: 028-12306

Pengshui Train Station
Changtan Township, Pengshui District
Phone: 028-12306

Qijiang Train Station
Qijiang
Phone: 028-12306

Qianjiang Train Station
Zhengyang Town, Qianjiang District
Phone: 028-12306

Rongchang Train Station
Xueyuan Rd, Rongchang County
Phone: 028-12306

Shapingba Train Station
Shapingba Zhandong Rd, Shapingba District
Phone: 028-12306

Tongnan Train Station
307 Provincial Rd, Tongnan District
Phone: 028-12306

Wanzhou Train Station
Longbao Town, Wanzhou District
Phone: 028-12306

Wulong Train Station
No.19, Furongdong, Xiangkou Town, Wulong County
Phone: 028-12306

Xiushan Train Station
Zhonghe Town, Xiushan County
Phone: 028-12306

Yongchuan Train Station
Huochezhan North Rd, Yongchuan
Phone: 028-12306

Youyang Train Station
Meishu Village, Longtan Town, Youyang
County
Phone: 028-12306

Train stations in Fujian Province
Train stations in Fuzhou Municipality

Lianjiang Train Station
Huawu Village, Jiangnan Township,
Lianjiang County, Fujian
Phone: 0591-63581892

Fuzhou Train Station
No.502, Hualin Road, Jin'an District,
Fuzhou, Fujian
Phone: 0591-87050222

Luoyuan Train Station

Baihua Village, Songshan Town, Luoyuan County, Fujian

Phone: 0591-63582192

Minqing Train Station

No.483, Meipu Village, Meixi Town, Minqing County, Fujian

Phone: 0591-87059470

Train stations in Longyan Municipality

Longyan Train Station

Renmin Road, Xinluo District, Longyan

Phone: 0597/3183189

Changting Train Station

Tingzhou Town, Changting County, Longyan

Phone: 0597/3167812

Yongding Train Station

Yongdingmen, Fengcheng Town, Yongding County, Longyan

Phone: 0597-3153912

Shanghang Train Station

Pingpu Village, Jiaoyang Township, Shanghang County, Longyan

Phone: 0597/3137212

Zhangping Train Station

Jingcheng Subdistrict, Zhangping City

Phone: 0597-3178866

Guanzhishan Train Station

Pengkou Town, Liancheng County, Longyan

Phone: 0597-3127512

Maiyuan Train Station

No.101, Biling South Road, Xinqiao Town, Zhangping City

Phone: 0598-8834252

Pinglin Train Station

Pinglin Village, Tieshan Town, Xinluo District, Longyan

Phone: 0597-3184512

Yanshi Train Station

Libang Village, Yanshi Town, Xinluo District, Longyan

Phone: 0597-3184612

Dashen Train Station

Dashen Village, Luzhi Township, Zhangping City

Phone: 0597-7760264

Banwei Train Station

Banwei Village, Yanshi Town, Xinluo District, Longyan

Phone: 0597-3184712

Suban Train Station

Suban Township, Xinluo District, Longyan

Phone: 0597-3184812

Jitai Train Station
Jitai Village, Xiyuan Township, Zhangping City
Phone: 0597-3184912

Train stations in Nanping Municipality

Nanping Train Station
No.49, Hengpai Road, Fujian
Phone: 0599-8627751

Nanping South Train Station
No.100, Gongye Road, Shuidong, Nanping, Fujian
Phone: 0599-8244376

Wuyishan Train Station
Zhanqian Road, Comprehensive Farm, Wuyishan City, Fujian
Phone: 0599-8352332

Shunchang Train Station

No.1, Huochang Road, Shuangxi Subdistrict, Shunchang County, Fujian

Phone: 0599-8277472

Shaowu Train Station

No.2, Jiefang West Road, Shaowu City, Fujian

Phone: 0599-8262742

Jianyang Train Station

Wulizhang Village, Tongyou Town, Jianyang City, Fujian

Phone: 0599-8353622

Jian'ou Train Station

Qilijie New Area, Jian'ou City, Fujian

Phone: 0599-8236022

Guangze Train Station

Pingshan Road, Guangze County, Fujian

Phone: 0599-8270652

Laizhou Train Station

No.3, Zhanqian Road, Laizhou Town, Nanping, Fujian

Phone: 0599-8245642

Train stations in Ningde Municipality

Ningde Train Station

Zhangwan Town Tuwei Village, Dongqiao Zone, Ningde, Fujian

Phone: 0591-63582442

Xiapu Train Station

Chi'an Village, Xiapu County, Fujian

Phone: 0591-63583242

Gutian Train Station

Huangtian Town, Gutian City, Fujian

Phone: 0593-3762966

Fuding Train Station

Danqi Village, Fuding City, Fujian

Phone: 0591-63583582

Fu'an Train Station

Wanwu Village, Fu'an City, Fujian

Phone: 0591-63582812

Tailaoshan Train Station

Qinyu Town, Fuding City, Fujian

Phone: 0591-63583432

Train stations in Quanzhou Municipality

Quanzhou East Train Station

Chengdong Subdistrict, Fengze District, Quanzhou

Phone: 0595-22642232

Anxi Train Station

Zhuanwen Village, Chengxiang Town, Anxi County, Quanzhou

Phone: 0595-23225033

Hutou Train Station

Hutou Town, Anxi County, Quanzhou
Phone: 0595-23401688

Changji Train Station
Changji Village, Bailai Township, Anxi County, Quanzhou
Phone: 0595-23182550

Xiaozhou Train Station
Futian Township Andu Village, Gande Town, Anxi County, Quanzhou
Phone: 0595-23173278

Nan'an Train Station
Meilin Subdistrict, Nan'an City
Phone: 0595-86271198

Jingu Train Station
Jingu Township, Anxi County, Quanzhou
Phone: 0595-23366814

Gekou Train Station

Futian Township Gekou Village, Gande Town, Anxi County, Quanzhou
Phone: 0595-23176436

Gande Train Station
Gande Township, Anxi County, Quanzhou
Phone: 0595-23166077

Fude Train Station
Fude Village, Gande Township, Anxi County, Quanzhou
Phone: 0595-23168831

Train stations in Sanming Municipality

Sanming Train Station
No.155, Gongye South Road, Sanyuan District, Sanming
Phone: 0598-8887292

Yong'an Train Station
No.1248, Yanjiang East Road, Yong'an City

Phone: 0598-8833622

Shaxian Train Station

Shiqiao Community, Fenggang Town, Shaxian

Phone: 0598-8857392

Train stations in Xiamen Municipality

Xiamen Train Station

No.900, Xiahe Road, Xiamen, Fujian

Phone: 0592-2038888

Train stations in Zhangzhou Municipality

Zhangzhou East Train Station

Guokeng Town, Longwen District, Zhangzhou

Phone: 0596-6366782

Hua'an Train Station

Huafeng Town, Hua'an County

Phone: 0596-6366642

Train stations in Gansu Province
Train stations in Baiyin Municipality

Baiyin Train Station

No.168, Jianshe East Road, Baiyin Municipality, Gansu

Phone: 0943-5984022

Baiyin West Train Station

Wangxian Township, Baiyin District, Baiyin Municipality, Gansu

Phone: 0943-5982222

Jingyuan Train Station

Jingyuan County, Baiyin Municipality Municipality, Gansu Province

Phone: 0943-5965112

Jingtai Train Station

Rd., Train Station of Jingtai County, Baiyin Municipality, Gansu
Phone: 0943-5984632

Changzheng Train Station
Pingchuan District, Baiyin Municipality Municipality, Gansu Province
Phone: 0943-5976324

Jingyuan West Train Station
Wulan Town, Jingyuan County, Baiyin Municipality, Gansu

Xingquanbao Train Station
Xingquanbao, Xiquan Township, Jingtai County, Baiyin Municipality, Gansu

Wujiachuan Train Station
Liuchuan Township, Jingyuan County, Baiyin Municipality, Gansu

Hongshaxian Train Station

Hongshaxian, Wuchuan Township, Baiyin District, Baiyin Municipality, Gansu

Dongwan Train Station

Dongwan Town, Jingyuan County, Baiyin Municipality, Gansu

Changcheng Train Station

Caowotan Town, Jingtai County, Baiyin Municipality, Gansu

Hongxiantai Train Station

Hongxiantai, Zhongquan Township, Jingtai County, Baiyin Municipality, Gansu

Train stations in Dingxi Municipality

Dingxi Train Station

No.336, Jiaotong Road, Anding District, Dingxi, Gansu

Phone: 0932-5977332

Longxi Train Station

Jiaotong Road, Longxi County, Dingxi, Gansu

Phone: 0932-5956222

Yuntianxiang Train Station

Yuntian Township, Longxi County, Dingxi, Gansu

Tong'anyi Train Station

Tong'anyi Township, Longxi County, Dingxi, Gansu

Train stations in Jiayuguan Municipality

Jiayuguan Train Station

No.1, Yingbin Road, Jingtieshan Zone, Jiayuguan Municipality, Gansu

Phone: 0937-5972222

Lvhua Train Station

Greening Street Block, Jiayuguan Municipality, Gansu

Phone: 0937-5973222

Chunfeng Train Station
Jiayuguan Municipality Municipality, Gansu Province

Train stations in Jinchang Municipality

Jinchang Train Station
Hexibao Town, Yongchang County, Jinchang, Gansu
Phone: 0935-5974222

Yushi Train Station
Hexibao Town, Yongchang County, Jinchang, Gansu

Jiling Train Station
Hexibao Town, Yongchang County, Jinchang, Gansu

Train stations in Jiuquan Municipality

Jiuquan Train Station

Xidong Town, Suzhou District, Jiuquan, Gansu

Phone:　　0937-5925422

Dunhuang Train Station

Mogao Town, Dunhuang City, Jiuquan, Gansu

Phone:　　0937-5959522

Qingshui Train Station

Qingshui Town, Suzhou District, Jiuquan, Gansu

Phone:　　0937-5925222

Guazhou Train Station

Yuanquan Town, Guazhou County, Jiuquan, Gansu

Phone:　　0937-5949422

Shulehe Train Station

Sandaogou Town, Guazhou County, Jiuquan, Gansu

Phone: 0937-5939222

Liuyuan Train Station

Liuyuan Town, Guazhou County, Gansu

Phone: 0902-7130222

Yumen Town Train Station

No.1, Changsheng Road, Yumen City, Gansu

Phone: 0937-5934519

Hedong Train Station

Hedong Township, Jiuquan, Gansu

Xiaoquan East Train Station

Guazhou County, Gansu Province

Xiakou Train Station

Guazhou County, Gansu Province

Shibandun Train Station

Guazhou County, Gansu Province

Hongliuhe Train Station
Guazhou County, Gansu Province

Daquan Train Station
Guazhou County, Gansu Province

Anbei Train Station
Guazhou County, Gansu Province

Qiaowan Train Station
Hedong Township, Jiuquan, Gansu

Zhaodong Train Station
Guazhou County, Gansu Province

Liugou Train Station
Bulongji Township, Guazhou County, Jiuquan, Gansu

Train stations in Lanzhou Municipality

Lanzhou Train Station
No.393, East Road, Train Station of Chengguan District, Lanzhou, Gansu
Phone: 0931–492222

Lanzhou East Train Station
Jiaojiawan, Chengguan District, Lanzhou, Gansu

Lanzhou West Train Station
Xijin West Road, Qilihe District, Gansu
Phone: 0931-2942222

Yongdeng Train Station
Yongdeng County, Lanzhou Municipality, Gansu Province
Phone: 0931-2986402

Haishiwan Train Station
Honggu District, Lanzhou Municipality, Gansu Province
Phone: 0971-7199222

Hekou South Train Station
Xincheng Town, Xigu District, Gansu
Phone: 0931-2940142

Xiaguanying Train Station
Xiaguanying Town, Yuzhong County, Lanzhou, Gansu
Phone: 0931-2980942

Shuiyuan Train Station
Water Source, Zhonghe Town, Gaolan County, Lanzhou

Shuichewan Train Station
Shuichewan, Honggu District, Lanzhou, Gansu

Shaojiatang Train Station
Shaojiatang, Zhonghe Town, Gaolan County, Lanzhou

Zhujiayao Train Station

Zhujiayao, Heishi Township, Gaolan County, Lanzhou

Fengshuicun Train Station

Fengshui Village, Shidong Township, Gaolan County, Lanzhou

Dongzicun Train Station

Dongzi Village, Honggu District, Lanzhou, Gansu

Bapanxia Train Station

Hekou Village, Xigu District, Lanzhou, Gansu

Huazhuang Train Station

Huazhuang, Honggu District, Lanzhou, Gansu

Podixia Train Station

Dongchuan Township, Xigu District, Lanzhou, Gansu

Luotuoxiang Train Station

Luotuo Alley, Laizibao Township, Yuzhong County, Lanzhou, Gansu

Longquansi Train Station

Longquansi, Longquansi Town, Yongdeng County, Lanzhou, Gansu

Lijiaping Train Station

Lijiaping, Longquan Township, Yuzhong County, Lanzhou, Gansu

Hewan Train Station

Hekou Village, Xigu District, Lanzhou, Gansu

Chenguanying Train Station

Chenping Township, Xigu District, Lanzhou, Gansu

Zhangjiaci Train Station

Zhangjiaci, Honggu District, Lanzhou, Gansu

Xujiatai Train Station

Xujiatai, Yuzhong County, Lanzhou, Gansu

Xigu城 Train Station

Xigu District, Lanzhou Municipality, Gansu Province

Wangjiawan Train Station

Wangjiawan, Gancaodian Town, Yuzhong County, Lanzhou, Gansu

Sangyuanzi Train Station

Sangyuanzi, Laizibao Township, Yuzhong County, Lanzhou, Gansu

Gancaodian Train Station

Gancaodian Town, Yuzhong County, Lanzhou, Gansu

Gaolan Train Station

Gaolan County, Lanzhou Municipality, Gansu Province

Phone: 0943-5984320

Train stations in Longnan Municipality

Liangdang Train Station

Zhan'erxiang Town, Liangdang County, Gansu

Phone: 029-96688688

Huixian Train Station

Jialing Town, Huixian, Gansu

Phone: 029-96688688

Hongqing Train Station

Xipo Town, Liangdang County, Gansu

Phone: 029-96688688

Train stations in Pingliang Municipality

Pingliang Train Station

Pingliang, Kongtong District, Pingliang, Gansu

Phone: 0933-5972222

Pingliang South Train Station

Xinli Village, Kongtong District, Pingliang, Gansu

Ankouyao Train Station

Baoping Road, Ankou Town, Huating County, Pingliang, Gansu

Phone: 029-96688688

Miaozhuang Train Station

Miaozhuang, Sishilipu Town, Kongtong District, Pingliang, Gansu

Xinli Train Station

Xinli Village, Kongtong District, Pingliang, Gansu

Chongxin Train Station

Tongcheng Town, Chongxin County, Pingliang, Gansu

Shenyuhe Train Station

Shenyuhe Township, Huating County, Pingliang, Gansu
Phone: 029-96688688

Train stations in Tianshui Municipality

Tianshui Train Station

No.2, East of First Highway, Maiji District, Tianshui, Gansu
Phone: 0938-4922222

Wushan Train Station

Dongshun Township, Wushan County, Tianshui, Gansu
Phone: 0938-4960072

Gangu Train Station

No.48, South of Road, Xinxing Town, Gangu County, Tianshui, Gansu
Phone: 0938-4950272

Xinyang Train Station

Xinyang Town, Maiji District, Tianshui, Gansu
Phone: 0938-4934892

Weinan Train Station

Weinan Town, Maiji District, Tianshui, Gansu
Phone: 0938-4934722

Yuanyang Train Station

Yuanyang Town, Wushan County, Tianshui, Gansu

Luomen Train Station

Luomen, Wushan County, Tianshui, Gansu

Nanhechuan Train Station

Shifo Township, Maiji District, Tianshui, Gansu

Hejiadian Train Station
Shandan Township, Wushan County, Tianshui, Gansu

Yuanlong Train Station
Yuanlong Town, Maiji District, Tianshui, Gansu
Phone: 029-96688688

Sanyangchuan Train Station
Weinan Town Township, Maiji District, Tianshui, Gansu

Train stations in Wuwei Municipality

Wuwei Train Station
No.64, Jiedaxin Road, Train Station of Liangzhou District, Wuwei, Gansu
Phone: 0935-5929222

Wuwei South Train Station

Wuweinan Town, Liangzhou District, Wuwei, Gansu
Phone: 0935–5922222

Tianzhu Train Station

Tianzhu Tibetan Aut. County, Wuwei Municipality, Gansu Province
Phone: 0931–2986502

Gulang Train Station

Dingning Town, Gulang County, Gansu
Phone: 0935-5924451

Tanjiajing Train Station

Haizitan Town, Gulang County, Wuwei, Gansu
Phone: 0935–5924604

Shixiazi Train Station

Zhenda Jingzhen, Gulang County, Wuwei, Gansu

Shangyaodun Train Station
Hedong Township, Liangzhou District, Wuwei, Gansu

Heichongtan Train Station
Dajing Town, Gulang County, Wuwei, Gansu

Yuandun Train Station
Hujiabian Township, Gulang County, Wuwei, Gansu

Tumenzi Train Station
Tumen Town, Gulang County, Wuwei, Gansu

Dachaigou Train Station
Dachaigou Town, Tianzhu Tibetan Aut. County, Wuwei, Gansu

Longgou Train Station
Heisongyi Town, Gulang County, Wuwei, Gansu

Huangyang Train Station

Huangyang Town, Wuwei, Gansu

Train stations in Zhangye Municipality

Zhangye Train Station

Zhenxi Road, Dongyuan, Ganzhou District, Zhangye, Gansu

Phone: 0936-5972222

Shandan Train Station

Qingquan Town, Shandan County, Gansu

Linze Train Station

Shahe Town, Linze County, Zhangye, Gansu

Phone: 0936–5975322

Gaotai Train Station

Nanhua Town, Gaotai County, Zhangye, Gansu

Phone: 0936–5975422

Jingtieshan Train Station

Domestic, Sunan County, Zhangye, Gansu

Phone: 0937–5975322

Dongshuixia Train Station

Domestic, Sunan County, Zhangye, Gansu

Xusanwan Train Station

Xinba Township, Gaotai County, Zhangye, Gansu

Pingyuanbao Train Station

Pingyuanbao Town, Ganzhou District, Zhangye, Gansu

Langweishan Train Station

Domestic, Sunan County, Zhangye, Gansu

Train Stations in Guangdong Province
Train Stations in Foshan Municipality

Foshan Train Station

No.30, Wenchang Road, Chancheng District, Foshan

Phone: 0757-82810543

Sanshui Train Station

No.1, Zhanqian Street, Sanshui District

Train Stations in Zhongshan

Zhongshan Train Station

G4W Guang'ao Expy, Zhongshan, Guangdong

Zhongshan North Train Station

Minying West Rd, Zhongshan, Guangdong

Guzhen Train Station

268 Provincial Road Side Rd, Zhongshan, Guangdong

Train Stations in Guangzhou Municipality

Guangzhou Train Station

No.159, Huanshi West Road, Guangzhou

Phone: 020-61357222

Guangzhou East Train Station

No.1, Dongzhan Road, Tianhe District, Guangzhou

Phone: 020-61346610

Guangzhou North Train Station

No.1, Zhanqian Road, Huadu District, Guangzhou

Phone: 020-61356850

Guangzhou West Train Station

No.5, Xiwan East Road, Liwan District, Guangzhou

Train Stations in Heyuan Municipality

Heyuan Train Station

Zhanqian Road, Jianshe Avenue (W.), Heyuan, Guangdong
Phone: 0762-2827832

Longchuan Train Station
Longchuan County, Guangdong Province
Phone: 0762-2825002

Heping Train Station
Heping County, Heyuan Municipality, Guangdong Province
Phone: 0762-2826172

Train Stations in Huizhou Municipality

Huizhou Train Station
Jiangbei, Huizhou, Guangdong
Phone: 0752-5823020

Train Stations in Zhaoqing

Zhaoqing Train Station
Zhanbei Road, Zhaoqing

Phone: 0758-6161822

Train Stations in Jieyang Municipality

Jieyang Train Station
Dongshan   District,   Jieyang   Municipality,
Guangdong Province
Phone: 0754-86358317

Train Stations in Maoming Municipality

Maoming Train Station
No.51, Youcheng First Road, Maoming
Phone: 0668-2326144

Maoming East Train Station
Zhanqian Fifth Road, Maoming
Phone: 0668-6568562

Huazhou Train Station
No.139, Zhanqian Road, Huazhou City

Train Stations in Meizhou Municipality

Meizhou Train Station

Binfang South Road, Meizhou, Guangdong

Phone: 0753-6136132

Dabu Train Station

Sanhe Town, Dabu County, Meizhou, Guangdong

Phone: 0753-6154569

Fengshun Train Station

Fengshun County, Guangdong Province

Phone: 0754-86358732

Xingning Train Station

Mochi, Xingnan Avenue, Xingning City, Guangdong

Phone: 0753-6156842

Train Stations in Qingyuan Municipality

Yingde Train Station

Dazhan Town, Yingde City

Phone: 0763-6826132

Yuantan Train Station

No.1, Yuejin Road, Yuantan Town, Qingcheng District, Qingyuan

Phone: 0763-3122280

Train Stations in Shantou Municipality

Shantou Train Station

Taishan Road, Shantou, Guangdong

Phone: 0754-86338172

Train Stations in Shaoguan Municipality

Shaoguan Train Station

Lianhua N Rd.

Shaoguan East Train Station

No.1, Zhannan Road, Zhenjiang District, Shaoguan

Phone: 0751-6172222

Lechang Train Station

No.50, Changshan East Road, Lechang City

Phone: 0751-6167122

Pingshi Train Station

Pingshi Town, Lechang City

Phone: 0751-6158167

Train Stations in Shenzhen Municipality

Shenzhen Train Station

No.1, Jianshe Road, Luohu District, Shenzhen

Phone: 0755-61382222

Shenzhen West Train Station

Xuefu West Road, Nanshan District

Phone: 0755-61380021   0755-61380053

Bantian Train Station

Bantian Village, Buji Town, Longgang District

Xili Train Station

Chaguang Road, Xili Town, Nanshan District

Pinghu Train Station

Pinghu Town, Shenzhen

Buji Train Station

Shenhui Road, Longgang District, Shenzhen

Train Stations in Dongguan

Dongguan Train Station

Changping Town, Dongguan

Phone: 0769-86272903

Dongguan East Train Station

Maiyuanxiang, Changping Town, Dongguan, Guangdong

Phone: 0769-5824982

Shilong Train Station

Shilong Town, Dongguan

Phone: 0769-86271732

Zhangmutou Train Station

Zhangmutou Town, Dongguan

Phone: 0769-86272482

Train Stations in Zhanjiang Municipality

Zhanjiang Train Station

No.40, Jiefang West Road, Xiashan District, Zhanjiang, Guangdong

Phone: 0759−3531562

Zhanjiang West Train Station

Diaosu Village, Mazhang District, Zhanjiang, Guangdong

Phone: 0759-6530532

Lianjiang Train Station

Dongsheng Road, Lianjiang City

Suixi Train Station
No.18, Wencang Road, Suixi County

Xuwen Train Station
Chengbei Zone, Xuwen County, Guangdong
Phone: 0759-6530232

Leizhou Train Station
Hongfu Village, Leizhou City, Guangdong
Phone: 0759-6530422

Hechun Train Station
Hechun Town, Lianjiang City

Train Stations in Yangjiang

Yangchun Train Station
YangchunCity

Chunwan Train Station

Yangchun City

Train Stations in Guizhou Province
Train Stations in Guiyang Municipality

Guiyang Train Station
No.1, Sitong Street, Nanming District, Guiyang
Phone: 028-12306

Xifeng Train Station
Xifeng County, Guiyang Municipality
Phone: 028-12306

Longli Train Station
Guiyang area
Phone: 028-12306

Pingba Train Station
Guiyang area
Phone: 028-12306

Huchao Train Station

Guiyang area
Phone: 028-12306

Train Stations in Liupanshui Municipality

Liupanshui Train Station
Liupanshui Municipality, Guizhou Province
Phone: 028-12306

Baiguo Train Station
Baiguo   Train   Station,   Baiguo   Town,
Panxian, Liupanshui, Guizhou
Phone: 0858-2191891

Songhe Train Station
Songhe Train Station, Panxian, Liupanshui,
Guizhou
Phone: 0858-2190708

Sanjiazhai Train Station
Sanjiazhai   Train   Station,   Shuicheng
County, Liupanshui, Guizhou

Phone: 0858-2190732

Panguan Train Station
Panguan Train Station, Duanjiang Town, Panxian, Guizhou
Phone: 0858-2191803

Maocaoping Train Station
Maocaoping Train Station, Shuicheng County, Liupanshui, Guizhou
Phone: 0858-2190762

Xiaoyugu Train Station
Xiaoyugu Train Station, Xiangshui Town, Panxian, Guizhou
Phone: 0858-2194412

Weiqing Train Station
Weiqing Train Station, Lemin Town, Panxian, Liupanshui, Guizhou
Phone: 0858-2194532

Liuzhi Train Station

Pingzhai, Liuzhite District
Phone:　　028-12306

Hongguo Train Station

Hongguo Train Station, Hongguo Town, Panxian, Liupanshui, Guizhou
Phone:　　0858-2191262

Train Stations in Tongren Municipality

Tongren Train Station

No.1, Qingshui North Road, Tongren City, Guizhou

Yuping Train Station

Yuping, Tongren, Guizhou

Mengxi Train Station

Mengxi Town, Songtao County, Guizhou

Train Stations in Zunyi Municipality

Zunyi Train Station

Zunyi Municipality

Phone:　　　028-12306

Tongzi Train Station

Tongzi County, Zunyi Municipality

Phone:　　　028-12306

Train Stations in Hainan Province
Train Stations in Directly–jurisdicted Cities & Counties of Hainan

Wanning Train Station

Jian She Lu Rd, Wan Ning Shi, Hainan

Dongfang Train Station

Dongfang City, Hainan Province

Lingshui Train Station

Lingshui, Hainan

Qionghai Train Station

Ai Hua Dong Lu Rd, Qiong Hai Shi, Hainan

Wenchang Train Station
Wenchang, Hainan

Dongfanghong Train Station
Train Station Neighbourhood, Dongfanghong Town
Phone: 0467-8152021

Train Stations in Haikou Municipality

Haikou Train Station
Yuehai Avenue, Xiuying District, Haikou, Hainan
Phone: 0898-31686222

Haikou East Train Station
Xiuying, Haikou, Hainan

Train Stations in Sanya Municipality

Sanya Train Station
Hairun Road, Sanya, Hainan

Phone: 0898-31887222

Train Stations in Hebei Province
Train Stations in Chengde Municipality

Chengde Train Station

No.235, Chezhan Road, Shuangqiao District, Chengde Municipality, Hebei

Chengde East Train Station

Taipingzhuang Village, Shuangqiao District, Chengde Municipality, Hebei

Yingshouyingzi Train Station

Yingshouyingzi Mining District, Chengde Municipality Municipality, Hebei

Luanping Train Station

No.164, West of Zhenxing Road, Luanping County, Chengde Municipality, Hebei

Longhua Train Station

No.8, Bei'an Road, Longhua County, Chengde Municipality, Hebei

Pingquan Train Station
Dongfang Street, Pingquan County, Chengde Municipality, Hebei

Siheyong Train Station
Siheyong Town, Weichang County, Chengde Municipality, Hebei
Phone: 0314-7690718

Jijiagou Train Station
Kelegou Town , Weichang Manchu-Mongol Aut. County, Hebei
Phone: 0476－2867432

Chaoyangdi Train Station
Chaoyangdi Town, Weichang County, Chengde Municipality, Hebei
Phone: 0476-2867342

Xinglong Train Station

Wuling Street, Xinglong County, Chengde Municipality, Hebei

Xinzhangzi Train Station

No.1, Xinda Hutong, Xinzhangzi Village, Chengde County, Chengde Municipality, Hebei

Xiaosigou Train Station

Nanwushijiazi Town, Pingquan County, Chengde Municipality, Hebei

Xiataizi Train Station

Xiatai Sub-station, Lijiaying Township, Xinglong County, Chengde Municipality, Hebei

Xiabancheng Train Station

No.1, Chezhan Road, Xiabancheng Town, Chengde County, Hebei

Shangbancheng Train Station

Xiejiaying Village, Development New Area, Shuangqiao District, Chengde Municipality, Hebei

Shangbancheng South Train Station

Shangban Urban, Development New Area, Chengde Municipality, Hebei

Beimaquanzi Train Station

Beimaquanzi Town, Yingshouyingzi Mining District, Chengde Municipality, Hebei

Panjiadian Train Station

Luanjiadian Village, Lijiaying Township, Xinglong County, Chengde Municipality, Hebei

Train Stations in Handan Municipality

Handan Train Station

No.2, Zhanqian Street, Hanshan District, Handan Municipality, Hebei

Shexian Train Station
Yingbin Street, Shexian, Handan Municipality, Hebei

Wu'an Train Station
No.256, Tiebei Road, Wu'an City, Hebei

Cixian Train Station
No.2, Youyi Road, Cixian, Hebei

Cishan Train Station
Zhongkongbi Village, Cishan Town, Wu'an City, Hebei

Kangcheng Train Station
Kangxi Village, Kangcheng Town, Wu'an City, Hebei

Jingdian Train Station
Xiazhuang, Jingdian Town, Shexian, Hebei

Yangyi Train Station
Yangyi Town, Wu'an City, Hebei

Train Stations in Hengshui Municipality

Hengshui Train Station
No.1, Center Street, Taocheng District, Hengshui, Hebei

Longhua Train Station
North of Hengde Road, Longhua Town, Jingxian, Hengshui, Hebei

Shenzhou Train Station
No.1, Taoyuan Street, Shenzhou City, Hengshui, Hebei

Raoyang Train Station
No.186, Fuqiang Street, Raoyang County, Hengshui, Hebei

Zaoqiang Train Station
Fuqiang Road (Middle Section), Zaoqiang County, Hengshui, Hebei

Qianmotou Train Station
Nantou, Shopping Street, Qianmotou Town, Shenzhou City, Hengshui, Hebei

Daying Train Station
Zhanqian Street, Daying Town, Zaoqiang County, Hengshui, Hebei

Train Stations in Langfang Municipality

Langfang Train Station
North End of Changfu Road, Anci District, Langfang, Hebei

Langfang North Train Station
No.55, Jiefangdao, Langfang, Hebei

Wen'an Train Station

Xiaowangdong Village, Daliu Town, Wen'an County, Langfang, Hebei

Gu'an Train Station
Xinyuan East Street, Gu'an County, Langfang, Hebei

Bazhou Train Station
Yingbinlu Train Station, Bazhou City, Hebei

Sanhe County Train Station
South of Fudong Road, Ju'an Residential Area, Sanhe City, Langfang, Hebei

Yanjiao Train Station
No.938, Jingyu Street, Yanjiao Development Area, Sanhe City, Langfang, Hebei

Train Stations in Qinhuangdao Provinces

Beidaihe Train Station

No.54, Zhannan Street, Beidaihe District, Qinhuangdao, Hebei

Funing Train Station

Tiegong Residential Area, 200m North of & 102 State Highway Cross Huandao, Yingbin Road, Funing County, Qinhuangdao, Hebei

Changli Train Station

South End of Minsheng Street, Changli County, Qinhuangdao, Hebei

Shanhaiguan Train Station

No.1, Nanguan Street, Shanhaiguan District, Qinhuangdao
Phone: 0335-7942242

Longjiaying Train Station

Longjiaying Village, Donggang Town, Haigang District, Qinhuangdao, Hebei

Train Stations in Shijiazhuang Municipality

Shijiazhuang Train Station
No.2, Daqiao Road, Xinhua District, Shijiazhuang, Hebei

Shijiazhuang North Train Station
No.1, Shizhuang Road, Xinhua District, Shijiazhuang, Hebei

Xinji Train Station
No.1, Xinghua Road, Xinji City, Hebei

Jinzhou Train Station
No.1, South Guangming Street, Cangshi Road, Jinzhou City, Shijiazhuang, Hebei

Gaoyi Train Station
No.53, Xinjian Street, Fengzhong Road, Gaoyi County, Shijiazhuang, Hebei

Gaocheng Train Station

No.97, Yong'an West Road, Gaocheng City, Shijiazhuang, Hebei

Jingxing Train Station

Weishui Town, Jingxing County, Shijiazhuang, Hebei

Yuanshi Train Station

No.32, Shengli Street, Yuanshi County, Shijiazhuang, Hebei

Jingnan Train Station

Nanyu Town, Jingxing County, Shijiazhuang, Hebei

Nanyu Train Station

Tianchang Town, Jingxing County, Shijiazhuang, Hebei

Train Stations in Tangshan Municipality

Tangshan Train Station

No.160, Xinhua W. Ave., Lubei District, Tangshan, Hebei

Tangshan North Train Station

No.1, Yingbin Road, Fengrun District, Tangshan, Hebei

Qian'an Train Station

400m West of Chengnanyou, Qian'an City, Tangshan, Hebei

Luanxian Train Station

North of State Highway 205 , Yanshan Street, Luanxian New Town, Tangshan, Hebei

Yutian Train Station

No.299, Huochang Road, Wuzhong Street, Yutian County, Tangshan, Hebei

Train Stations in Xingtai Municipality

Xingtai Train Station

No.20, Chezhan North Road, Xingtai Municipality, Hebei

Nangong East Train Station

Duanlutou Town, Nangong City, Xingtai, Hebei

Shahe Train Station

No.12, Baiyun Road, Shahe City, Hebei

Qinghecheng Train Station

No.1, Zhanqian Street, Qinghe County, Xingtai Municipality, Hebei

Train Stations in Zhangjiakou Municipality

Zhangjiakou Train Station

No.1, Dong'an Street, Qiaodong District, Zhangjiakou, Hebei

Zhangjiakou South Train Station

No.11, Zhanqian West St., Hi-and-New Tech Park of Zhangjiakou, Hebei

Xuanhua Train Station

No.1, Chezhan Street, Xuanhua District, Zhangjiakou, Hebei

Xiahuayuan Train Station

No.7, Highway Street, Xiahuayuan Zone, Zhangjiakou, Hebei

Guanting Train Station

Guanting Town, Huailai County, Zhangjiakou, Hebei

Shacheng Train Station

Shacheng Town, Huailai County, Zhangjiakou, Hebei

Jiuzhuangwo Train Station

Guanting Town, Huailai County, Zhangjiakou

Train Stations in Henan Province
Train Stations in Luohe Municipality

Luohe Train Station

Gong'an Street, Luohe, Henan

Phone: 0395-5962222

Train Stations in Luoyang Municipality

Luoyang Train Station

No.1, South of Road, Xigong District, Luoyang

Phone: 0379-62561222

Luoyang East Train Station

No.38, Datong Street, Chanhe District, Luoyang

Phone: 0379-62722222

Ruyang Train Station

Da'an Village, Industrial Park of Ruyang County

Phone: 0375-7125532

Yanshi Train Station

No.8, Chezhan Road, Yanshi, Henan

Phone: 0379–65365991

Guanlin Train Station

Dadong Village, Luolong District, Luoyang

Phone: 0379-62729147

Xin'an Train Station

No.39, South of Qinhuang Road, Xin'an County, Henan

Phone: 0379–62640789

Baihe Train Station

Baihe Village, Baihe Town, Mengjin County

Phone: 0379-62041542

Mengjin Train Station

Xinzhuang Village, Songzhuang Township, Mengjin County

Phone: 0379-62041519

Liuzhuang Train Station

Madong Village, Jili District, Luoyang

Phone: 0391-2183612

Train Stations in Nanyang Municipality

Nanyang Train Station

No.3, Tiedong Street, Wolong District, Nanyang, Henan

Phone: 0377-63082222

Nanzhao Train Station

Yunyang Town, Nanzhao County, Henan

Phone: 0377-63084104

Dengzhou Train Station

Dengzhou City, Hena

Phone: 0377-63096114

Tongbai Train Station

Tongbai County, Henan

Phone: 0377-68828120

Zhenping Train Station

Jiankang Road, Zhenping County, Henan

Phone: 0377-65088601

Xixia Train Station

Xixia County, Henan

Phone: 0377-65109019

Tanghe Train Station

Tanghe County, Henan

Phone: 0377-68818382

Neixiang Train Station

Neixiang County, Henan

Phone: 0377-65068765

Train Stations in Puyang Municipality

Taiqian Train Station

West of Deshang Highway, Taiqian County, Henan

Phone: 0393-2699312

Train Stations in Sanmenxia Municipality

Sanmenxia Train Station
No.5, East of Huanghe Road, Sanmenxia, Henan
Phone: 0398-2583122

Sanmenxia West Train Station
Yuandian Town, Shanxian, Sanmenxia, Henan
Phone: 0398-2571422

Lingbao Train Station
No.1, Chezhan Road, Lingbao City, Henan
Phone: 0398-2569157

Yima Train Station
Yima City, Henan Province
Phone: 0398-2534452

Mianchi Train Station

Mianchi County, Henan Province
Phone: 0398-2552252

Train Stations in Shangqiu Municipality

Shangqiu Train Station
No.59, Zhanqian Road, Shangqiu
Phone: 0370-2992222

Shangqiu South Train Station
East End of Nanjing Road, Shangqiu
Phone: 0370-2997205

Minquan Train Station
Heping   West   Road,   Minquan   County,
Shangqiu
Phone: 0370-2990408

Ningling Train Station
Liuhe Town, Ningling County, Shangqiu
Phone: 0370-2990251

Yucheng Train Station

Yucheng, Yucheng County, Henan

Phone: 0370-2914772

Xiayi Train Station

Xiayi, Chezhan Town, Xiayi County, Henan

Phone: 0370-2914642

Train Stations in Xinyang Municipality

Xinyang Train Station

No.115, 'erqi South Street, Pingqiao District, Xinyang

Phone: 0376-6224114

Shangcheng Train Station

Train Station Development Area, Shangshiqiao Township, Shangcheng County, Henan

Phone: 0376-6829550

Xinxian Train Station

Development Area, Jingjiulu Train Station, Xinji Town, Xinxian, Henan
Phone: 0713-2105872

Xixian Train Station

Lidian Village, Caohuanglin Township, Xixian, Henan
Phone: 0376－6828003

Luoshan Train Station

Chengnan, Luoshan County, Henan
Phone: 0376－6828250

Huangchuan Train Station

Train Station Development Area, Huangchuan County, Xinyang, Henan
Phone: 0376-6829302

Huaibin Train Station

Caipo Village, Langan Town, Huaibin County, Henan
Phone: 0376-6829262

Gushi Train Station

Yaolaojia Village, Duanji Township, Gushi County, Henan

Phone: 0376-6829841

Minggang Train Station

Minggang Train Station, Xinyang, Henan

Phone: 0522-66215

Train Stations in Xinxiang Municipality

Xinxiang Train Station

No.1, Pingyuan Road, Xinxiang Municipality

Phone: 0373-2122222

Weihui Train Station

No.138, Xiangyu Avenue, Weihui City

Phone: 0373-2179174

Changyuan Train Station

Bo'ai Road, Changyuan County

Phone: 0373-2151262

Huojia Train Station
Huojia County, Henan Province
Phone: 0391-2125814

Train Stations in Xuchang Municipality

Xuchang Train Station
No.2, Chezhan Road, Weidu District, Xuchang Municipality
Phone: 0374-2588222

Changge Train Station
No.103, Chezhan Street, Changge County, Xuchang Municipality
Phone: 0374-2584818

Train Stations in Zhengzhou Municipality

Zhengzhou Train Station
No.82, Second Highway, Er'qi District, Zhengzhou
Phone: 0371-68352222

Gongyi Train Station

Guangming Road, Gongyi City, Henan

Phone: 0371-8534512

Zhongmou Train Station

No.1, Dongfeng Road, Zhongmou County

Phone: 0371-68374842

Train Stations in Zhoukou Municipality

Zhoukou Train Station

Chezhan Road, Zhoukou, Henan

Phone: 0394-6179977; 6178569

Train Stations in Zhumadian Municipality

Zhumadian Train Station

No.1, Jiefang Road, Zhumadian, Henan

Phone: 0396-3930114

Queshan Train Station

Train Station of Queshan County, Henan

Phone: 0396-2590347

Suiping Train Station
Train Station of Suiping County, Henan
Phone: 0396-2565739

Xiping Train Station
Train Station of Xiping County, Henan
Phone: 0396-6236528

Train Stations in Qiandongnan Miao–Dong Aut. Prefecture

Zhenyuan Train Station
Group 8, Xixiu Street, Zhenyuan
Phone: 028-12306

Shibing Train Station
Tunshang   Village,   Yangliutang   Town,
Shibing County
Phone: 028-12306

Kaili Train Station

No.88, Qingjiang Road, Kaili City
Phone:　　028-12306

Train Stations in Qiannan Buyei–Miao Aut. Prefecture

Guiding Train Station
Hehua Community, Chengguan Town, Guiding County
Phone:　　028-12306

Fuquan Train Station
Bishan Road, Machangping Town, Fuquan City
Phone:　　028-12306

Dushan Train Station
Zhemian Village, Mawei Town, Dushan County
Phone:　　028-12306

Duyun Train Station

Wangjiasi Village, Xiaoweizhai Town, Duyun City

Phone: 028-12306

Guiding South Train Station

Changming Town, Guiding County

Phone: 028-12306

Mawei Train Station

Yujiawan, New Town Zone, Mawei Town

Phone: 028-12306

Train Stations in Qianxinan Buyei–Miao Aut. Prefecture

Xingyi Train Station

No.5, Baiyun Road, Dingxiao Development Area, Xingyi City, Guizhou

Phone: 0859-2282222

Ceheng Train Station

Qiaoma Town, Ceheng County, Guizhou

Weishe Train Station

Weishe Town, Xingyi City, Guizhou

Phone: 0859-2284232

Train Stations in Hong Kong

Lo Wu Station
Lo Wu Station Rd, Kowloon, Hong Kong
Phone: +852 2881 8888

Jingjiu Railway on the Chinese mainland is connected with Hong Kong MTR (Mass Transit Railway Corporation) East Rail at Lo Wu Station in Kowloon.

Train stations in India

Train stations in Andhra Pradesh Province

Guntur Train Station

Guntur, Andhra Pradesh 522002, India

Hyderabad Train Station

Public Garden Rd, Devi Bagh, Red Hills, Nampally, Hyderabad, Andhra Pradesh 500004, India

Kazipet Train Station

Rahamatnagar, Kazipet, Andhra Pradesh 506003, India

Nellore Train Station

Achri St, Kapatipalem, Santhapet, Nellore, Andhra Pradesh 524001, India

Rajahmundry Train Station

Main Rd, Alcot Gardens, Rajahmundry, Andhra Pradesh 533101, India

Secunderabad Train Station
Railway Officer Colony, Botiguda, Boiguda, Hyderabad, Andhra Pradesh 500025, India

Tirupati Train Station
Tirupati Rd, Royal Nagar, Tirupati, Andhra Pradesh 517501, India

Vijayawada Train Station
Vijayawada, Andhra Pradesh 520001, India

Vishakapatnam Train Station
Railway Quarters, Mahaarajupeta, Visakhapatnam, Andhra Pradesh 530004, India

Warangal Train Station
Station Rd, Shiva Nagar, Warangal, Andhra Pradesh 506002, India

Train Stations in Assam Province

Dibrugarh Town Train Station

RKB Path, Dibrugarh, Assam 786001, India

Guwahati Train Station

Station Rd, Mawhati, Paltan Bazaar, Guwahati, Assam 781001, India

Silchar Train Station

Tarapur, Silchar, Assam 788003, India

Train Stations in Bihar Province

Barauni Train Station

Baro, Bihar 851210, India

Begu Sarai Train Station

National Highway 31, Sarvodaya Nagar, Begusarai, Bihar 851101, India

Bhagalpur Train Station
Bhikhanpur, Bhagalpur, Bihar 812002, India

Buxar Train Station
Mitralok Colony, Buxar, Bihar 802101, India

Chhapra Train Station
Railway Colony, Chapra, Bihar 841301, India

Darbhanga Train Station
Kathalbari, Darbhanga, Bihar 846004, India

Gaya Train Station
Railway station Rd, Jagdeo Nagar, Gol Bagicha, Gaya, Bihar 823002, India

Hajipur Train Station

Pedestrian Overpass, Hajipur, Bihar 844102, India

Kathiar Train Station
Railway Colony, Katihar, Bihar 854105, India

Muzaffarpur Train Station
Sutapatti, Pokhraira, Muzaffarpur, Bihar 842001, India

Patna Train Station
Pedestrian Overpass, Mithapur Farm Area, Mithapur, Patna, Bihar 800000, India

Siwan Train Station
Station Rd, Railway Quarters, Siwan, Bihar 841226, India

Train Stations in Chandigarh Province

Chandigarh Train Station
Chandigarh, 160102, India

Train Stations in Chhattisgarh Province

Bilaspur Train Station

Tarbahar Chowk, Bilaspur, Chhattisgarh 495004, India

Durg Train Station

Durg, Chhattisgarh 491001, India

Raigarh Train Station

Agrasen Colony, Raigarh, Chhattisgarh 496001, India

Raipur Train Station

Foot Bridge, Raipur, Chhattisgarh 492009, India

Train Stations in Delhi

H Nizamuddin Train Station

Nizamuddin, Humayun's Tomb, Nizamuddin East, New Delhi, Delhi 110022, India

New Delhi Train Station

New Delhi, Delhi 110006, India

Train Stations in Goa

Madgaon Train Station

Sanscar Society, Margao, Goa 403601, India

Vasco da Gama Train Station

Swatantra Path, Vaddem, New Vaddem, Vasco da Gama, Goa 403802, India

Train Stations in Gujarat

Ahmedabad Train Station

Laxmi Bazar, Saraspur Ahmedabad, Gujarat 380002, India

Rajkot Train Station

Railway Station Rd, Junction Plot, Rajkot, Gujarat 360001, India

Surat Train Station

Station Rd, Suryapur Gate, Patel Nagar, Surat, Gujarat 395003, India

Vadodara Train Station

Maharaja Sayajirao University, Alkapuri, Vadodara, Gujarat 390020, India

Vapi Train Station

Imran Nagar, Vapi, Gujarat 396191, India

Train Stations in Haryana Province

Ambala Cantt Train Station

Ambala Cantt, Ambala City, Haryana 133001, India

Ambala City Train Station

Old Town, Ambala City, Haryana 134001, India

Faridabad Train Station

St Nagar, Sector 20A, Faridabad, Haryana 121003, India

Kalka Train Station
Azad Colony, Kalka, Haryana 133302, India

Panipat Train Station
Model Town, Panipat, Haryana 132108, India

Rohtak Train Station
Railway Colony, Naya Padav, Rohtak Station Diary Mohalla, Rohtak, Haryana 124001, India

Sonipat Train Station
Sonipat, Haryana 131304, India

Train Stations in Himachal Pradesh Province

Simla Train Station

Cart Rd, Nabha, Shimla, HP 171004, India

Train Stations in Jammu & Kashmir Province

Jammu Train Station

Transportnagar, Jammu, JK 180012, India

Train Stations in Jharkhand Province

Bokaro Steel City Train Station

Bokaro Thermal, Jharkhand 829107, India

Dhanbad Train Station

Pandey Muhalla, Dhanbad, Jharkhand 826001, India

Hatia Train Station

Pedestrian Overpass, Hatia Railway Colony Type II, Maharatoli, Ranchi, Jharkhand 834004, India

Ranchi Train Station

Lower Chutia, Samlong, Ranchi, Jharkhand 834001, India

Ranchi Road Train Station

Ranchi Road Railway Station Rd, Ranchi Rd, Ramgarh, Jharkhand 829117, India

Tatanagar Train Station

Khasmahal, Jugsalai, Jamshedpur, Jharkhand 831007, India

Train Stations in Karnataka Province

Bangalore Train Station

Gubbi Thotadappa Rd, Railway Colony, Sevashrama, Bangalore, Karnataka 560023, India

Bangarapet Train Station

Amaravathy Nagar, Bangarapet, Karnataka 563114, India

Belgaum Train Station

Shastri Nagar, Shahapur, Belgaum, Karnataka 590001, India

Bellary Train Station

BSNL Colony, Devi Nagar, Bellary, Karnataka 583101, India

Bijapur Train Station

Railway Station Area, Bijapur, Karnataka 586104, India

Dharwar Train Station

Dharwad, Karnataka 580007, India

Gulbarga Train Station

Pedestrian Overpass, Ghouse Nagar, Tarfile, Gulbarga, Karnataka 585102, India

Hubli Train Station

Mantur Rd, Railway Colony, Hubli, Karnataka 580023, India

Mangalore Train Station
Foot Overbridge, Attavar, Mangalore, Karnataka 575001, India

Mysore Train Station
Medar Block, Yadavagiri, Mysore, Karnataka 570001, India

Train Stations in Kerala Province

Alleppey Train Station
Pedestrian Overpass, Kunnumpuram, Alappuzha, Kerala 688012, India

Alwaye Train Station
Railway Station Rd, Periyar Nagar, Aluva, Kerala 683101, India

Calicut Train Station
Kuttichira, Kozhikode, Kerala 673001, India

Cochin Train Station

Willingdon Island, Kochi, Kerala 682003, India

Ernakulam Train Station

Xavier Arakkal Rd, Ayyappankavu, Ernakulam, Kerala 682018, India

Kottayam Train Station

Nagampadam, Kottayam, Kerala 686002, India

Palghat Train Station

Railway Station Rd, Kallekkulangara, Chepilamury, Akathethara, Palakkad, Kerala 678002, India

Quilon Train Station

Chamkkada,Kollam, Kerala 691001, India

Trichur Train Station

Railway Station Rd, Veliyannur, Thrissur, Kerala 680021, India

Trivandrum Train Station

Chalai Bazaar, Thampanoor, Thiruvananthapuram, Kerala 695001, India

Train Stations in Madhya Pradesh Province

Bhopal Train Station

Navbahar Colony, Bhopal, Madhya Pradesh 462001, India

Bina Train Station

Bina Station Footover Bridge, Bina, Madhya Pradesh 470113, India

Gwalior Train Station

LNUPE Campus, Thatipur, Gwalior, Madhya Pradesh 474002, India

Indore Bg Train Station

Chhoti Gwaltoli, Indore, Madhya Pradesh 452007, India

Itarsi Train Station

Foot Over Bridge, Venkatesh Colony, Itarsi, Madhya Pradesh 461122, India

Jabalpur Train Station

Tagore Railway Colony, Civil Lines, Jabalpur, Madhya Pradesh 482001, India

Katni Train Station

Gayatri Nagar, Katni, Madhya Pradesh 483501, India

Ratlam Train Station

Station Rd, Bapu Nagar, Ratlam, Madhya Pradesh 457001, India

Satna Train Station

Railway Station Rd, Railway Colony, Satna, Madhya Pradesh 485001, India

Ujjain Train Station

Pedestrian Overpass, Malipura, Ujjain, Madhya Pradesh 456006, India

Train Stations in Maharashtra Province

Akola Train Station

Jafrabad, Akola, Maharashtra 444001, India

Amravati Train Station

Maltekdi, Amravati, Maharashtra 444606, India

Aurangabad Train Station

Silk Mill Colony, MIDC, Aurangabad cantonment, Maharashtra, India

Bhusaval Train Station

Gandhi Nagar, Gadkari Nagar, Bhusawal, Maharashtra 425201, India

Gondia Train Station

Bhim Nagar, Rail Toli, Gondia, Maharashtra 441601, India

Manmad Train Station

Maharashtra State Highway 10, Ahmed Nagar, Manmad, Maharashtra 423104, India

Mumbai Train Station

Dadal Estate, Bane Compound, Tardeo, Mumbai, Maharashtra 400008, India

Nagpur Train Station

Sitabuldi, Nagpur, Maharashtra 440001, India

Nanded Train Station

Railway Station Rd, Harsh Hagar, Nanded, Maharashtra 431601, India

Nasik Train Station

Rajwada Nagar, Deolali Goan, Nashik, Maharashtra 422101, India

Pune Train Station

HH Prince Aga Khan Rd, Agarkar Nagar, Pune, Maharashtra, 411001, India

Ratnagiri Train Station

Maharashtra 415639, India

Sangli Train Station

Vishrambag, Sangli, Maharashtra 416416, India

Solapur Train Station

Laxmi Vishnu Chawl, Solapur, Maharashtra 413002, India

Thane Train Station

Station Rd, Shivaji Nagar, Thane West, Thane, Maharashtra 400601, India

Wardha Train Station

Major State Highway 3, Stationfail, Wardha, Maharashtra 442001, India

Train Stations in Odisha Province

Bhubaneshwar Train Station
Master Canteen Chowk, Ashok Nagar, Bhubaneshwar, Odisha 751009, India

Cuttack Train Station
Gandharpur, Cuttack, Odisha 753003, India

Puri Train Station
Puri, Odisha 752002, India

Rourkela Train Station
Udit Nagar, Rourkela, OD 769001, India

Train Stations in Punjab Province

Amritsar Train Station
Guru Arjun Nagar, Putli Ghar, Amritsar, Punjab 143002, India

Bhatinda Train Station

Railway Colony, Partap Nagar, Bathinda, Punjab 151001, India

Jalandhar City Train Station
Jalandhar, Punjab 144001, India

Ludhiana Train Station
Gandhi Nagar, Civil Lines, Ludhiana, Punjab 141001, India

Patiala Train Station
Patiala, Punjab 147003, India

Train Stations in Rajasthan Province

Abu Road Train Station
MDR 49, Railway Colony Abu Rd, Rajasthan, India

Ajmer Train Station

Jaipur Rd, Patel Nagar, Topdara Ajmer, Rajasthan 305001 India

Alwar Train Station

Naru Marg, Indira Colony, Alwar, Rajasthan 301001, India

Bikaner Train Station

Bikaner, Rajasthan 334001, India

Jaipur Train Station

Railway Rd, Shanti Nagar, Civil Lines, Jaipur, Rajasthan 302008, India

Jaisalmer Train Station

Industrial Area, Gandhi Nagar, Jaisalmer, Rajasthan 345001, India

Jodhpur Train Station

Ratanada, Jodhpur, Rajasthan 342001, India

Kota Train Station

Kota Railway Foot Over Bridge, Railway Colony, Railway Station Area, Kota, Rajasthan 324002, India

Udaipur Train Station

Jawahar Nagar, Central Area, Udaipur, Rajasthan 313001, India

Train Stations in Tamil Nadu Province

Chennai Train Station

EVR Periyar Salai, Park Town, Chennai, Tamil Nadu 600 003, India

Coimbatore Train Station

Pedestrian Overpass, Gopalapuram, Coimbatore, Tamil Nadu 641001, India

Erode Train Station

Erode Railway Colony, Erode, Tamil Nadu 638002, India

Kanyakumari Train Station
Kanyakumari, Tamil Nadu 629702, India

Katpadi Train Station
Katpadi Jct, Dharapadavedu, Katpadi, Tamil Nadu 632007, India

Madurai Train Station
Junction Overpass, Southern Railway Colony, Madurai, Tamil Nadu 625016, India

Rameswaram Train Station
Rameshwaram, Tamil Nadu 623526, India

Salem Train Station
Town Railway Station Rd, Maravaneri, Salem, Tamil Nadu, 636001, India

Sivakasi Train Station

Velayutham Rd, Sengamala Nachiar Puram, Sivakasi, Tamil Nadu 626123, India

Tenkasi Train Station

Tenkasi, Tamil Nadu 627811, India

Thanjavur Train Station

Parisutham Nagar, Thanjavur, Tamil Nadu 613007, India

Tiruchirapalli Train Station

Devathanam, Tiruchirappalli, Tamil Nadu 620002, India

Tirunelveli Train Station

Balabagya Nagar South, Tirunelveli Junction, Tirunelveli, Tamil Nadu 627001, India

Tuticorn Train Station

West Shanmugapuram, Thoothukudi, Tamil Nadu 628001, India

Train Stations in Uttar Pradesh Province

Agra Cantt Train Station

Idgah Colony, Agra, Uttar Pradesh 282001, India

Agra City Train Station

Gadhapura, Civil Lines, Agra, Uttar Pradesh 282003, India

Agra Fort Train Station

State Highway 39, Agra Fort, Rakabganj Agra, Uttar Pradesh 282003, India

Aligarh Train Station

Church Compound, Civil Lines, Aligarh, Uttar Pradesh 202001, India

Allahabad Train Station

Civil Lines, Allahabad, Uttar Pradesh 211001, India

Amethi Train Station
Railway Station Rd, Amethi, Uttar Pradesh 227405, India

Azamgarh Train Station
Musapur, Azamgarh, Uttar Pradesh 276001, India

Bahraich Train Station
Friganj, Bahraich, Uttar Pradesh 271801, India

Ballia Train Station
Harpur Middhi Rd, Ballia, Uttar Pradesh 277001, India

Bareilly Train Station
Station Rd, Civil Lines, Bareilly, Uttar Pradesh 243001, India

Basti Train Station

Jamohara, Basti, Uttar Pradesh 272002, India

Faizabad Train Station

Railway Colony - Station Rd, Railway Colony, Faizabad, Uttar Pradesh 224001, India

Farukhabad Train Station

Thandi Sadak Station Rd, Devrampur, Farrukhabad, Uttar Pradesh 209625, India

Ghaziabad Train Station

Pedestrian Overpass, Bhur Bharat Nagar, Railway Colony, Madhopura, Ghaziabad, Uttar Pradesh 201009, India

Gorakhpur Train Station

Station Rd, Kawwa Bagh Colony, Gorakhpur, Uttar Pradesh 273012, India

Jhansi Train Station

Pedestrian Overpass, Rani Laxmi Nagar, Jhansi, Uttar Pradesh 284003, India

Kanpur Train Station

Jaipuria Rd, Dhana Khori, Mirpur, Kanpur, Uttar Pradesh 208004, India

Lucknow Train Station

Jawahar Nagar, Qaiserbagh, Lucknow, Uttar Pradesh 226018, India

Mathura Train Station

Mathura Junction (west) Access Road, Shanti Nagar, Mathura, Uttar Pradesh 281001, India

Mau Train Station

Railway Line Rd, Railway Colony, Mau, Uttar Pradesh 275101, India

Meerut City Train Station

Meerut Cantt, Meerut, Uttar Pradesh 250002, India

Moradabad Train Station

Malviya Nagar, Budh Bazaar, Moradabad, Uttar Pradesh 244001, India

Mughal Sarai Train Station

Mughal Sarai, Uttar Pradesh 232101, India

Rae Bareli Train Station

PNT Colony, Raebareli, Uttar Pradesh 229001, India

Saharanpur Train Station

Lakdi Ka Pul, Subhash Nagar, Saharanpur, Uttar Pradesh 247001, India

Varanasi Train Station

Jalalipura, Varanasi, Uttar Pradesh 221001, India

Train Stations in Uttarakhand Province

Dehradun Train Station
Lakkhi Bagh, Dehradun, Uttarakhand 248001, India

Haridwar Train Station
Purusharthi Market Rd, Shikhu Pur, Devpura, Haridwar, Uttarakhand 249401, India

Kathgodam Train Station
Kathgodam, Haldwani, Uttarakhand 263126, India

Rishikesh Train Station
Adarsh Nagar, Ganga Nagar, Rishikesh, Uttarakhand 249201, India

Roorkee Train Station
Railway Station Rd, Bhagirath Kunj, Roorkee, Uttarakhand 247667, India

Train Stations in West Bengal Province

Asansol Train Station

Station Rd, Railpar, Asansol, West Bengal 713301, India

Barrackpore Train Station

Local Rd, Barrackpore, West Bengal 700120, India

Burdwan Train Station

Railway Loco Colony, Bardhaman, West Bengal 713103, India

Chittaranjan Train Station

Chittaranjan, West Bengal 815354, India

Darjeeling Train Station

Hill Cart Rd, Limbugaon, Darjeeling, West Bengal 734101, India

Howrah Train Station

Howrah Goods Yard, Howrah Railway Station, Howrah, West Bengal 711101

Kharagpur Train Station

Kharagpur, West Bengal 721301, India

Kolkata Train Station

Belgachia, Kolkata, West Bengal 700037, India

Malda Town Train Station

English Bazar, West Bengal 732101, India

New Jalpaiguri Train Station

Nawapara, Siliguri, West Bengal 734004, India

Train Stations in Indonesia
Jakarta

Ancol Train Station

Benyamin Sueb, 10710, Jakarta, Jakarta Special Capital Region

Duri Train Station

Jl. Kali Nayar 1 Rd, Jakarta

Gambir Train Station

Jalan Medan Merdeka Timur no. 1, Jakarta Pusat

Gondangdia Train Station

Srikaya 1 Rd, Jakarta

Jakarta Kota Train Station

Jalan Stasiun Kota no.1, Jakarta

Jatinegara Train Station

Bekasi Barat Raya Street, Jatinegara, East Jakarta

Kampung Bandan Train Station

Kampung, WTC Mangga Dua, Jakarta

Klender Train Station

Jalan Bekasi Timur Raya Klender Street, Klender, Duren Sawit, Jakarta Timur, DKI Jakarta

Manggarai Train Station

Jalan Manggarai Utara No. 1 Jakarta Selatan

Pasar Minggu Train Station

Jalan Raya Pasar Minggu Street, Kota Jakarta, Selatan 12510

Pasar Senen Train Station

Jalan Let. Jen. Suprapto-Kramat, Bunder

Sudirman Train Station

Sudirman Rd, Menteng, Central Jakarta

Tanah Abang Train Station

Jalan Jatibaru Street, Kampung Bali, Tanah Abang

Tanjung Priok Train Station

Jalan Laksamana R. E. Martadinata Street, Kota Jakarta

Banten

Parung Panjang Train Station

Parung Panjang, Bogor, Indonesia

Rangkasbitung Train Station

Jalan Stasiun No.1, Rangkasbitung, Lebak, Banten

Serang Train Station

Jalan Kitapa No. 2 Cimuncang, Serang Municipality, Banten Province

Serpong Train Station
Jalan Nn Street, Serpong, South Tangerang, Banten

Tangerang Train Station
Ki-Asnawi Street, Tangerang, Banten

West Java

Bandung Train Station
Kebon Kawung St., Bandung, West Java

Ciroyom Train Station
Arjuna Street, Andir, Bandung

Kiaracondong Train Station
Jalan Kiaracondong Street, Bandung, West Java

Banjar Train Station

Jalan Banjar-Pangandaran Rd, Banjar, West Java

Bekasi Train Station

Stasiun Bekasi Rd, Bekasi, West Java

Bogor Train Station

Nyi Raja Permas Street, Bogor, West Java

Cianjur Train Station

Jalan Yusuf Hasiru Street, Cianjur, West Java

Cikampek Train Station

Jalan A. Yani Rd, Cikampek, West Java

Cirebon Kejaksan Train Station

Siliwangi Street, Kebonbaru, Kejaksan, Cirebon

Cirebon Prujakan Train Station

Nyi Mas Gandasari Street, Pekalangan, Pekalipan district, Cirebon

Depok Train Station
Stasiun Street, Jabodetabek, Depok, West Java

Jatibarang Train Station
Jalan Mayor Sangun Street, Jatibarang, Indramayu, West Java

Karawang Train Station
Jalan Arif Rahman Hakim Street, Karawang, West Java

Padalarang Train Station
Jalur Cikampek-Padalarang Rd, Bandung, West Java

Purwakarta Train Station
Jalan Singawinata St, Purwakarta, West Java

Rancaekek Train Station
Rancaekek, West Java

Tasikmalaya Train Station

Jalan Stasiun Street, Tasikmalaya, West Java

Central Java

Cepu Train Station

Jalan Diponegoro, Cepu, Central Java

Cilacap Train Station

Jalan Swadaya, Cilacap, Central Java

Klaten Train Station

Jalan Kopral Sayom Street, Klaten, Central Java

Kroya Train Station

Jalan Stasiun Rd, Kroya, Central Java

Kutuarjo Train Station

Jalan Stasiun Kutoarjo St, Kutuarjo, Central Java

Pekalongan Train Station

Jalan Merdeka Rd, Pekalongan, Central Java

Purwokerto Train Station

Purwokerto, Central Java

Semarang Tawang Train Station

Jalan Raya Semarang-Purwodadi Rd, Semarang Poncol, Central Java

Solo Balapan Train Station

Jalan Gajah Mada Rd, Solo Balapan, Central Java

Lempuyangan Train Station

Jalan Lempuyangan St, Yogyakarta, Central Java

Yogyakarta Tugu Train Station

Jalan Pasar Kembang St, Yogyakarta, Central Java

East Java

Bangil Train Station
Jalan Gajah Mada St, Bangil, East Java

Banyuwangi Train Station
Banyuwangi, East Java

Blitar Train Station
Jalan Mastrip Rd, Blitar, East Java

Bojonegoro Train Station
Jalan Gajah Mada St, Bojonegoro, East Java

Jember Train Station
Jalan Wijaya Kusuma St, Jember, East Java

Jombang Train Station

Jalan Raya Ngrandu Perak St, Jombang, East Java

Kediri Train Station
Jalan Stasiun St, Kediri, East Java

Kertosono Train Station
Kertosono, East Java

Lamongan Train Station
Jalan Lamongrejo St, Lamongan, East Java

Madiun Train Station
Jalan Kompol Sunaryo St, Madiun, East Java

Malang Train Station
Jalan Trunojoyo St, Malang, East Java

Nganjuk Train Station
Jalan Yogyakarta-Sidoarjo St, Nganjuk, East Java

Pasuruan Train Station
Jalan Stasiun St, Pasuruan, East Java

Probolinggo Train Station
Jalan Ikan Paus St, Probolinggo, East Java

Sidoarjo Train Station
Jalan Stasiun St, Sidoarjo, East Java

Surabaya Gubeng Train Station
Jalan Stasiun Gubeng Surabaya St, Surabaya, East Java

Surabaya Kota Train Station
Jalan Stasiun Kota St, Surabaya, East Java

Surabaya Pasar Turi Train Station
Jalan Semarang St, Surabaya, East Java

Wonokromo Train Station

Jalan Stasiun Wonokromo St, Wonokromo, East Java

Sumatra

Medan Station Train Station

Jalan Stasiun Kereta Api St, Medan, Sumatra

Train Stations in Iran

Ahvaz Train Station
Sepah Rd, Ahvaz
Phone: 332021- 7

Andimeshk Train Station
Taleqani St, Andimeshk

Arak Train Station
Arak Village

Bandar Abbas Train Station
Bandar Abbas City
Phone: 29881

Damghan Train Station
Damghan City, Semnan Province

Esfahan Train Station
Esfahan City
Phone: 6876753

Firuzkuh Train Station

Firuzkuh City

Gorgan Train Station

Gorgan, Ostan-e Golestan

Jolfa Train Station

Jolfa County, East Azerbaijan Province

Karaj Train Station

Karaj, Alborz

Kashan Train Station

Molla Sodra Blvd

Phone: 98 361 446 0010

Kerman Train Station

Kerman City

Phone: 98 341 211 0762

Mashad Train Station

Mashhad, Khorasan Razavi
Phone: 98 511 200 4429

Pol-e Sefid Train Station
Pol-e Sefid City, Savadkuh County, Mazandaran Province

Qazvin Train Station
Qazvin City, Qazvin Province

Qom Train Station
Istgah St, Qom City
Phone: 98 251 441 7151, 98 251 661 7141

Sabzevar Train Station
Sabzervar City, Razavi Khorasan Province

Salmas Train Station
Azarbayjan-e Gharbi

Sarakhs Train Station
Sarakhs County, Razavi Khorasan Province

Shiraz Train Station
Fars Province

Shushtar Train Station
Shushtar County, Khuzestan Province

Tabriz Train Station
Rahohan Sq, Tabriz
Phone: 444 4419

Tehran Train Station
Rah-Ahan Sq, Valiasr Street
Phone: 98 21 5121

Torbat-e Heydarieh Train Station
Torbat-e Heydarieh County, Razavi Khorasan Province

Yazd Train Station
Rah Ahan Sq., Yazd

Zahedan Train Station

Motahhari, Zahedan

Zanjan Train Station
Khayam St., Zanjan

Train Stations in Iraq

The Iraqi Republic Railway Company (IRR) covers over approximately 1,900 km (1,200 miles). There are only 2 train stations open to public currently and a few others under construction.

Al Maqal Train Station
Al Ma'qil, Basrah

Baghdad Central Train Station
14th of July St, Baghdad

Train Stations in Israel

For more information about train stations and train schedule in Israel you should call at the Israeli Railway call center: *5770, 077-2324000.

Train Stations in Central District

Be'er Ya'akov Train Station
Simcha Holzberg St., Be'er Ya'akov

Beit Yehoshua Train Station
West of Moshav Bet Yehoshua, close to Poleg Interchange

Hod Hasharon Train Station
Sokolov Street, between Hod Hasharon & Kfar Saba

Kfar Saba - Nordau Train Station
Nordau Street

Lod Train Station
Yoseftal Ave., Southern Industrial Estate

Modi'in Train Station
1 HaHashmonaim Blvd.

Netanya Train Station
5 HaRakevet Way, Old Industrial Estate

Paatei Modi'in Train Station
Highway 431, opposite Ispro Centre

Petah Tikva Kiryat Aryeh Train Station
Em HaMoshavot Way, Stadium St.

Petah Tikva Segula Train Station
Yarkonim Junction, adjoining Yarkonim Trading Centre

Ramla Train Station
1 Eli Cohen St., southern city approach, behind Central Bus Station

Rehovot Train Station

Herzl St., Adjoining Weizmann Institute, Science-Based Industries Estate

Rishon LeZion - HaRishonim Train Station

Rishon LeZion - Nes Ziona road

Rishon LeZion Moshe Dayan Train Station

Moshe Dayan St. - Rishon LeTsiyyon, near the Cinema-City site

Rosh HaAyin North Train Station

To the north-west of Kessem Interchange, adjoining Afek National Park

Yavne Train Station

HaMeisav St., adjoining local market

Yavne West Train Station

Yavne

Train Stations in Haifa District

Atlit Train Station
Harduf St., HaRakevet Quarter, West Atlit

Binyamina Train Station
HaMesilla St., Binyamina Industrial Estate

Caesarea-Pardes Hanna Train Station
1 Bazelet St., Kesariyya Industrial Park

Hadera Ma'arav (West) Train Station
Train rd. Street, next to Sella Neighborhood

Kiryat Motzkin Train Station
Between Bar-Ilan St. & AHY Eilat St.

Train Stations in the Jerusalem District

Beit Shemesh Train Station
HeHarash St.

Jerusalem Malha Train Station
Yitzhak Moda'i Way, Malha area

Train Stations in North District

Acre Train Station
David Remez St.

Nahariya Train Station
2 HaGaaton Blvd., adjoining Central Bus
Station

Train Stations in Southern District

Ashdod Ad Halom Train Station
Menahem Begin Blvd., adjoining southern
city approach

Ashkelon Train Station
Adjoining Cosmos area, Kefar Silver
Junction

Be'er Sheva Central Train Station

8 Ben-Zvi St.

Be'er Sheva North Train Station
Ben-Gurion Way, 3rd Quarter

Dimona Train Station
HaMelacha St., adjoining Industrial Estate

Kiryat Gat Train Station
Continuance Cheshvan St

Lehavim Rahat Train Station
Lehavim West

Sderot Train Station
Sderot City

Train Stations in Tel Aviv District

Bat Yam-Komemiyut Train Station
Independence St. - Bat Yam

Bat Yam-Yoseftal Train Station

Yoseftal St. - Bat Yam, near Yoseftal Intersection on Ayalon road

Ben Gurion Airport Train Station
Terminal 3, Ben-Gurion Airport
Phone: 972 3-975-5555

Bnei Brak Train Station
1 Mivtsa Kadesh St., Bne Brak Industrial Estate

Herzliya Train Station
Ben-Zion Michaeli St., Shivat HaKochavim Ave. entrance

Holon Junction Train Station
Near Holon Junction

Holon-Wolfson Train Station
Wolfson St. - Holon, near Wolfson hospital

Tel Aviv HaHagana Train Station

32 HaHagana Way, adjoining HaTikva Quarter

Tel Aviv HaShalom Train Station
10 Givat HaTahmoshet St., adjoining Azrieli Mall

Tel Aviv Savidor Central Train Station
10 Al Parashat Derachim St. (continuation of Arlosoroff St.)

Tel Aviv University Train Station
95 Rokah Blvd., adjoining Rokah Interchange, opposite Trade Fairs Centre

Train Stations in Japan
Train Stations in Aichi Province

Age Train Station

Taketoyo, Chita District

Agui Train Station

Agui, Chita District

Aichi-Mito Train Station

Tokaido Main Line of Central Japan Railway Company in Toyokawa

Aichidaidagukumae Train Station

Toyoshashi

Aichikyuhaku-Kinen-Koen Train Station

Nagakute

Anjo Train Station

Tokaido Main Line of Central Jpan Railway Company in Anjo

Aoyama Train Station (Aichi)

Meitetsu's Kowa Line in Hnda

Arahata Train Station

Showa-Ku, Nagoya

Aratama-bashi Train Station

Mizuho-Ku, Nagoya

Arimatsu Train Station

Midori-Ku Nagoya

Asahi-mae Train Station

Meitetsu's Seto Line , Owariasahi

Asakura Train Station (Aichi)

Meitetsu's Tokoname Line, Chita

Biwajima Train Station

Kiyosu

Central Japan International Airport Train Station

Tokoname, Aichi

Chayagasaka Train Station

Chikusa-Ku, Nagoya

Chikusa Train Station

Higashi-ku and Chikusa-Ku , Nagoya

Chiryu Train Station

Chiryu

Phone: 566-81-0577

Cita-Handa Train Station

Handa, Aichi

Chita-Okuda Train Station

Mihama, Chita District

Chita-Taketoyo Train Station

Taketoyo, Chita District

Chukyo keibajo mae Train Station
Midori-Ku, Nagoya

Daidocho Train Station
Minami Ward, Nagoya, Aichi

Fujigaoka Train Station
Meito-Ku Nagoya
Phone: 45-901-4969

Fuki Train Station
Taketoyo, Chita District
Phone: 569-72-0311

Fukiage Train Station (Aichi)
Chikusa-Ku, Nagoya, Aichi Prefecture

Fushimi Train Station (Aichi)
Naka-Ku Nagoya

Gokiso Train Station
Showa-Ku, Nagoya

Hatta Train Station
Nakamura-Ku, Nagoya

Heian-dori Train Station
Kita-Ku, Nagoya

Higashi Betsuin Train Station
Naka-Ku, Nagoya

Higashi Kariya Train Station
Tokaido Main Line, Kariya

Higashiyama Koen Train Station
Chikusa-Ku, Nagoya

Hongo Train Station (Aichi)
Meito-Ku, Nagoya

Honjin Train Station
Nakamura-Ku, Nagoya

Horita Train Station
Mizuho-Ku, Nagoya

Hoshigaoka Train Station

Chikusa-Ku, Nagoya

Hotei Train Station

Konan

Phone: 568-61-5300

Ikeshita Train Station

Chikusa-Ku, Nagoya

Imaike Train Station

Chikusa-Ku, Nagoya, Aichi

Inazawa Train Station

Tokaido Main Line, Inazawa, Aichi

Inuyama Train Station

Inuyama, Aichi

Phone: 568-61-5300

Iwakura Train Station

Meitetsu Inuyama Line, Iwakura

Jimokuji Train Station
Meitetsu Tsushima Line, Ama

Jingu-mae Train Station
Nagoya Railroad, Atsuta-Ku, Nagoya

Kachigawa Train Station
Kasugai, Aichi

Kami-Otai Train Station
Nishi-Ku, Nagoya
52-502-9278

Kamimaezo Train Station
Naka-Ku, Nagoya

Kanayama Train Station
Naka-Ku and Atsuta-Ku, Nagoya

Kariya Train Station
Kariya, Aichi

Kashiwamori Train Station
Meitetsu Inuyama Line, Fuso

Kasugai Train Station
Kasugai, Aichi

Ko Train Station (Aichi)
Meitetsu Nagoya Line and Toyokawa Line,
Toyokawa

Komaki Train Station
Komaki
Phone: 568-76-2257

Konomiya Train Station
Meitetsu Nagoya Main Line, Inazawa

Train Stations in Akita Province

Akita Shinkansen Train Station
Tokyo and Akita in Akita Prefecture

Oiwake Train Station
Ou Main Line, Akita

Omagari Train Station
Daisen

Okubo Train Station
Ou Main Line, Katagami

Higashi-Noshiro Train Station
Noshiro, Akita

Train Stations in Aomori Province

Aomori Train Station
Aomori, Aomori

Hachinohe Train Station
Hachinohe, Aomori

Hirosaki Train Station
Hosanaki, Aomori

Train Stations in Chiba Province

Abiko Train Station
Abiko, Chiba

Anegasaki Train Station
Anegasaki, Ichihara, Chiba
Phone: 436-62-6631

Awa-Kamogawa Train Station
Central Kamogawa, Chiba

Chiba Train Station
Chiba, Chiba

Chiba-Minato Train Station
Mihama, Chiba

Choshi Train Station
Choshi, Chiba

Funabashi Train Station
Funabashi, Chiba

Goi Train Station

Ichihara, Chiba

Higashi-Matsudo Train Station

Matsudo, Chiba

Ichikawa Train Station

Ichikawa, Chiba

Ichikawa-Mama Train Station

Ichikawa, Chiba

Ichikawa-Shiohama Train Station

Ichikawa, Chiba

Kaihin-Makuhari Train Station

Mihama, Chiba

Kashiwa Train Station

Kashiwa, Chiba

Keisei Funabashi Train Station

Funabashi, Chiba

Keisei Narita Train Station
Narita, Chiba

Keisei Tsudanuma Train Station
Narashion Chiba

Keisei-Sakura Train Station
Sakura, Chiba

Keisei-Usui Train Station
Sakura, Chiba

Kisarazu Train Station
Kisarazu, Chiba

Kita-Narashino Train Station
Funabashi, Chiba
Phone: 47-465-3020

Mabashi Train Station
Matsudo, Chiba

Phone: 271-0051

Maihama Train Station
Urayasu, Chiba

Matsudo Train Station
Matsudo, Chiba

Minami-Nagareyama Train Station
Nagareyama, Chiba

Mobara Train Station
Mobara, Chiba

Nagareyama-Otakanomori Train Station
Nagareyama, Chiba

Train Stations in Ehime Province

Onishi Train Station
Imabari

Train Stations in Fukui Province

Awaraonsen Train Station
Hokuriku Main Line, Awara

Fukui Train Station
Fukui

Fukuiguchi Train Station
Fukui, Fukui Prefecture

Tsuruga Train Station
Tsuruga, Fukui
Phone: 770-22-0004

Train Stations in Fukuoka Province

Akasaka Train Station
Chuo-Ku, Fukuoka

Chihaya Train Station
Higashi-Ku, Fukuoka

Chikugo-Funagoya Train Station

Chikugo, Fukuoka

Chikushi Train Station
Chikushino, Fukuoka

Chikuzen-Maebaru Train Station
Itoshima, Fukuoka

Daizenji Train Station
Kurume

Hakata Train Station
Hakata
Phone: 092-431-0202

Hanabatake Train Station
Kurume, Fukuoka

Kashii Train Station
Higashi

Kokura Train Station
Kokura Kita, Kitakyushu

Kurosaki Train Station
Yahata Nishi, Kitakyushu

Kurume Train Station
Kurume

Meinohama Train Station
Nishi, Fukuoka

Minami-Fukuoka Train Station
Hakata
Phone: 92-511-5517

Nakasu-Kawabata Train Station
Hakata
Phone: 92-431-0202

Nishitetsu Fustsukaichi Train Station
Chikushino
Phone: 92-517-7095

Nishitetsu Kurume Train Station

Kurume

Phone: 942-47-2051

Nishitetsu Ogori Train Station

Ogori

Omuta Train Station

Omuta

Phone: 944-52-0052

Orio Train Station

Yahatanishi, Kitakyushu

Phone: 93-691-0024

Train Stations in Fukushima Province

Aizu-Wakamatsu Train Station

Aizuwakamatsu

Fukushima Train Station

Fukushima

Koriyama Train Station

Koriyama
Phone: 50-3736-7261

Nishi-Wakamatsu Train Station
Aizuwakamatsu

Shin-Shirakawa Train Station
Nishigo, Nishishirakawa

Train Stations in Gifu Province

Gifu Train Station
Gifu

Gifu-Hashima Train Station
Hashima, Gifu

Kasamatsu Train Station
Kasamatsu, Hashima District

Nakatsugawa Train Station
Nakatsugawa

Rokken Train Station

Kakamigahara

Shin-Kano Train Station

Kakamigahara

Shin-Naka Train Station

Kakamigahara, Gifu

Phone: 58-380-0304

Shin-Unuma Train Station

Kakamigahara, Gifu

58-384-0142

Tarui Train Station

Tarui, Fuwa District

Train Stations in Gunma Province

Doai Train Station

Minakami, Gunma

Gokan Train Station

Joetsu Line, Minakami

Itakura Toyodai-mae Train Station
Tobu Nikko Line, Itakura

Kawamata Train Station
Tob Isesaki Line, Meiwa
276-84-2154

Kuragano Train Station
Takasaki, Gunma

Minakami Train Station
Joetsu Line, Minakami

Takasaki Train Station
Yashimachi, Takasaki

Tatebayashi Train Station
Tobu Isesaki Line, Tatebayashi

Train Stations in Hiroshima Province

Fukuyama Train Station

Fukuyama, Hiroshima

Hiroshima Train Station

Minami, Hiroshima

Phone: 082-567-8011

Kure Train Station

Kure Line, Kure

Mihara Train Station

Mihara, Hiroshima

Phone: 848-62-4770

Miyoshi Train Station

Miyoshi, Hiroshima

Nishi-Hiroshima Train Station

Koi-honmachi, Nishi-Ku

Shin-Inokuchi Train Station

Inokuchi, Nishi

Yokogawa Train Station
Yokogawa, Nishi

Train Stations in Hokkaido Province

Ainosato-Kyokudai Train Station
Kita, Sapporo

Asahikawa Train Station
Asahikawa, Hokkaido

Bus Center-Mae Train Station
Chuo, Sopporo

Chitose Train Station
Chitose, Hokkaido

Fukuzumi Train Station
Chuo, Sapporo

Gryokaku Train Station
Hakodate
Phone: 138-41-3745

Hakodate Train Station
Hakodate, Hokkaido
Phone: 138-23-3085

Hassamu-Chuo Train Station
Nishi, Sapporo

Higashi-Kuyakusho-Mae Train Station
Higashi, Sapporo

Hoshioki Train Station
Teine, Sapporo

Inaho Train Station
Teine, Sapporo

Inazumi-Koen Train Station
Teine, Sapporo

Jieitai-Mae Train Station
Minami, Sapporo

Kami-Nopporo Train Station
Atsubetsu, Sapporo

Kikusui Train Station
Shiroishi, Sapporo

Train Stations in Hyogo Province

Aioi Train Station
Aioi, Hyogo

Akashi Train Station
Akashi

Amagasaki Train Station (Hanshin)
Amagasaki, Hyogo
6-6411-0281

Amagasaki Train Station (JR West)
Amagasaki, Hyogo

Amagasaki Center Pool-mae Train Station
Amagasaki, Hyogo

Hibarigaoka-Hanayashiki Train Station
Takarazuka

Hyogo Train Station
Hyogo-Ku, Kobe

Itayado Train Station
Suma, Kube
Phone: 78-732-7360

Kwanishi-Noseguchi Train Station
Kawanishi
Phone: 72-758-9806

Kinosaki Onsen Train Station
Toyooka, Kinosaki

Koshienguchi Train Station
Nishinomiya

Train Stations in Ibaraki Province

Inada Train Station
Kasama

Ishioka Train Station
Ishioka

Mito Train Station
Mito, Ibaraki

Train Stations in Ishikawa Province

Kanazawa Train Station
Kanazawa, Ishikawa

Train Stations in Iwate Province

Akabuchi Train Station
Shizukuishi

Arayashimmachi Train Station
Hachimantai

Ashigase Train Station

Tono, Iwate

Fujine Train Station
Kitakami

Hiraizumi Train Station
Hiraizumi, Nishiiwai
Phone: 191-46-2301

Hizume Train Station
Shiwa

Ichinohe Train Station
Ichinohe, Ninohe

Iwanebashi Train Station
Tono

Iwate-Numakunai Train Station
Iwate, Iwate Prefecture

Kadonohama Train Station
Hirono,Kunohe

Kintaichi-Onsen Train Station
Ninohe

Koma Train Station
Tamayama, Morioka

Kuji Train Station
Hachinohe Line, Kuji

Mataki Train Station
Ichinoseki

Matsuo-Hachimantai Train Station
Hachimantai

Mizusawa-Esashi Train Station
Oshu, Iwate

Morioka Train Station
Morioka
Phone: +81 19-622-3456

Niitsuki Train Station
Ichinoseki

Ofunato Train Station
Ofunato

Rikuchu-Yagi Train Station
Hirono, Kunohe

Yahaba Train Station
Yahaba, Shiwa

Train Stations in Kagawa Province

Ayagawa Train Station
Ayagawa, Ayauta

Kawaramachi Train Station
Takamatsu

Train Stations in Kagoshima Province

Chosa Train Station
Aira, Kagoshima

Hayato Train Station
Kirishima

Hiroki Train Station
Kagoshima

Ijuin Train Station
Hioki

Jigenji Train Station
Kagoshima

Kagoshima-Chuo Train Station
Kagoshima

Kokubu Train Station
Kirishima, Kagoshima

Ryugamizu Train Station

Kagoshima

Train Stations in Kanagawa Province

Ashigara Train Station
Odawara

Azamino Train Station
Aoba, Yokohama
Phone: 45-0901-4969

Bandobashi Train Station
Naka, Yokohama

Byobugaura Train Station
Isogo, Yokohama

Chuo-Rinkan Train Station
Yamato

Ebina Train Station
Ebina

Futako-Shinchi Train Station
Takatsu, Kawasaki

Hama-Kawasaki Train Station
Kawasaki, Kawasaki

Hashimoto Train Station
Midori, Sagamihara

Higashi-Kanagawa Train Station
Kanagawa, Yokohama

Higashi-Totsuka Train Station
Totsuka, Yokohama

Hiyoshi Train Station
Kohoku, Yokohama

Hon-Atsugi Train Station
Atsugi

Izumi-chuo Train Station
Izumi, Yokohama

Izumino Train Station
Izumi, Yokohama

Kajigaya Train Station
Takatsu, Kawasaki

Kamihoshikawa Train Station
Hodogaya, Yokohama

Kaminagaya Train Station
Konan, Yokohama

Kamiooka Train Station
Konan, Yokohama

Kanazawa-Hakkei Train Station
Kanazawa, Yokohama

Katase-Enoshima Train Station
Fujisawa

Keikyu Tsurumi Train Station

Tsurumi, Yokohama

Kozu Train Station
Odawara

Musashi-Mizonokuchi Train Station
Takatsu, Kawasaki

Train Stations in Kochi Province

Kochi Train Station
Kochi

Train Stations in Kumamoto Province

Kumamoto Train Station
Nishi, Kumamoto
Phone: 096-352-0212

Shiroshi Train Station
Ashikita, Kumamoto

Yatsushiro Train Station

Yatsushiro

Train Stations in Kyoto Province

Ayabe Train Station

Ayabe

Chushoma Train Station

Fushimi, Kyoto

Demachiyanagi Train Station

Sakyo, Kyoto

Fukuchiyama Train Station

Fukuchiyama

Kamitobaguchi Train Station

Fushimi, Kyoto

Kawaramachi Train Station

Shimogyo

Nagaoka-Tenjin Train Station
Nagaokakyo

Nishi-Kyogoku Train Station
Ukyo, Kyoto

Tofukuji Train Station
Higashiyama, Kyoto

Yamazaki Train Station
Oyamazaki, Otokuni District
Phone: 0586-23-2714

Train Stations in Mie Province

Ageki Train Station
Inabe

Aoyamacho Train Station
Iga, Mie
Phone: 0595-52-0039

Edobashi Train Station

Tsu, Mie

Ise-Wakamatsu Train Station

Suzuka

Kamayama Train Station

Kameyama

Kashikojima Train Station

Shima

Kintetsu Yokkaichi Train Station

Yokkaichi

Kuwana Train Station

Kuwana

Toba Train Station

Toba, Mie

Train Stations in Miyagi Province

Kita-Yobancho Train Station
Aoba, Sendai

Train Stations in Miyazaki Province

Miyakonojo Train Station
Miyakonojo
Phone: 0986-23-3954

Totoro Train Station
Nobeoka

Train Stations in Nagano Province

Amori Train Station
Nagano

Hirata Train Station
Matsumoto

Hitoichiba Train Station
Azumino

Imai Train Station

Nagano

Inariyama Train Station

Nagano

Kamishiro Train Station

Hakuba, Kitaazumi District

Karuizawa Train Station

Karuizawa, Kitasaku District

Kawanakajima Train Station

Nagano

Komoro Train Station

Aioicho, Komoro

Matsumoto Train Station

Matsumoto

Nishi-Ueda Train Station

Ueda, Nagano

Sakaki Train Station
Sakaki, Hanishina District

Shiojiri Train Station
Shiojiri

Tatsuno Train Station
Tatsuno, Kamiina District

Tokamachi Train Station
Tokamachi

Ueda Train Station
Ueda, Nagano

Yashiro Train Station
Chikuma

Train Stations in Nagasaki Province

Matsuura Train Station

Matsura

Omura Train Station

Omura

Sasebo Train Station

Sasebo

Phone: 0856-22-7115

Urakami Train Station

Kawaguchi, Nagasaki

Phone: 095-844-1554

Train Stations in Nara Province

Gakken Kit-Ikoma Train Station

Ikoma

Goido Train Station

Kashiba, Nara

Phone: 0745-79-0078

Ikoma Train Station
Ikoma
Phone: 0743-74-2056

Kashiharajingu-mae Train Station
Kashihara

Narayama Train Station
Nara

Shin-Omiya Train Station
Nara
Phone: 06-6771-3105

Tsubosakayama Train Station
Takatori, Takaichi

Yamato-Yagi Train Station
Kashihara, Nara

Yoshino Train Station
Yoshino, Yoshino District

Yoshinoguchi Train Station

Gose, Nara

Train Stations in Nigata Province

Higashi-Niigata Train Station

Higashi, Niigata

Maroshi Train Station

Gosen

Train Stations in Oita Province

Ozai Train Station

Oita

Yufuin Train Station

Yufuin, Oita

Phone: 0977-84-2021

Train Stations in Okayama Province

Bitchu-Kojiro Train Station
Niimi

Kiyone Train Station
Tsukubo, Soja

Train Stations in Okinawa Province

Naha-Kuko Train Station
Naha, Okinawa
Phone: 098-859-2630

Omoromachi Train Station
Naha

Shuri Train Station
Naha

Train Stations in Osaka Province

Abeno Train Station
Abeno, Osaka

Bentencho Train Station
Minato

Fuse Train Station
Higashiosaka
Phone: 06-6783-2260

Gamo-yonchome Train Station
Joto, Osaka

Hanaten Train Station
Tsurumi

Imamiya Train Station
Naniwa

Shuntokumichi Train Station
Higashiosaka

Kuzuha Train Station
Kuzuha, Hirakata

Phone: 080-9120-2510

Minami-Ibaraki Train Station
Ibaraki

Train Stations in Saga Province

Arita Train Station
Arita, Nishimatsuura
Phone: 0955-42-2820

Saga Train Station
Saga City
Phone: 0952-24-4029

Train Stations in Saitama Province

Bushi Train Station
Iruma, Saitama
Phone: 04-2932-0085

Hanno Train Station

Hanno

Phone: 042-972-2056

Higashi-Hanno Train Station

Hanno

Higashi-Tokorozawa Train Station

Tokorozawa

Kita-Asaka Train Station

Asaka

Kita-Sakado Train Station

Sakado

Phone: 049-282-0033

Kuki Train Station

Kuki, Saitama

Miyahara Train Station

Kita

Nshi-Tokorozawa Train Station
Tokorozawa

Sayamashi Train Station
Sayama
Phone: 04-2952-2156

Shiki Train Station
Niiza
Phone: 048-471-0047

Toda Train Station
Toda

Tsurugashima Train Station
Tsurugashima
Phone: 049-285-0033

Urawa Train Station
Urawa

Wakaba Train Station

Sakado
Phone: 049-284-1133

Train Stations in Shiga Province

Ishiyama Train Station
Otsu

Omi-Imazu Train Station
Takashima

Otsu Train Station
Otsu
Phone: 0668544129

Train Stations in Shimane Province

Gotsu Train Station
Gotsu

Yasugi Train Station
Yasugi

Train Stations in Shizuoka Province

Abekawa Train Station
Suruga, Shizuoka
Phone: 050-3772-3910

Fuji Train Station
Fuji

Hamamatsu Train Station
Naka, Hamamatsu
Phone: 08041705195

Ito Train Station
Ito, Shizuoka

Numazu Train Station
Numazu

Shizuoka Train Station
Aoi, Shizuoka

Train Stations in Tochigi Province

Kuroiso Train Station
Nasushiobara

Tobu Nikko Train Station
Nikko
Phone: 0288-54-0137

Train Stations in Tokushima Province

Sabase Train Station
Kaiyo, Kaifu

Train Stations in Tokyo Province

Ikebukuro Train Station
Toshima
Phone: 08041586299

Machida Train Station
Machida, Tokyo

Phone: +81 42-725-1611

Shimo-Kitazawa Train Station
Setagaya
Phone: +813-3468-2012

Tokyo Train Station
Chiyoda, Tokyo

Train Stations in Tottori Province

Babasakicho Train Station
Sakaiminato

Train Stations in Toyama Province

Inotani Train Station
Toyama

Takaoka Train Station
Takaoka

Toyama Train Station

Toyama

Train Stations in Wakayama Province

Gobo Train Station

Gobo, Wakayama

Phone: 0738-22-0395

Train Stations in Yamagata Province

Imaizumi Train Station

Nagai

Kita-Yamagata Train Station

Yamagata

Nagai Train Station

Nagai

Shinjo Train Station

Shinjo
Phone: 0233-22-5580

Yamagata Train Station
Yamagata

Train Stations in Yamaguchi Province

Yamaguchi Train Station
Yamaguchi City
Phone: 023-631-2131

Train Stations in Yamanashi Province

Enzan Train Station
Koshu

Yamanashi Train Station
Yamanashi

Train Stations in Kazakhstan

For more information about Kazakhstan you can call the Kazakhstan Railway office:

Help Line: +7 (7172) 93-01-13

Hotline: +7 (7172) 60-40-70

Central office Passenger transport: + 7 (7172) 600-200

Aktau Train Station

Stanciya Mangyshlak, N/n, Vokzalnaya Str., 130000, Aktau

Phone: 46 52 50

Aktobe Train Station

No. 22, Privokzalnaya Str., 030000, Aktobe

Phone: + 7 (7132) 105, 97-53-59, 21-17-77

Aktogay Train Station

Ayagoz District, East Kazakhstan Province

Almaty-I Train Station

Stancionnaya St., 1, Almaty

Phone: 296-17-90, 296-33-92

Almaty-II Train Station
Abylai Khan Av., h. 1 , Almaty
Phone: + 7 (727) 105, 296-15-44, 296-55-44, 296-53-44

Atyrau Train Station
1, Vokzalnaya Str., 060000, Atyrau
Phone: +7 (7122) 955-549, 955-116

Astana Train Station
1, 314-th Strelkovaya Diviziya Str., 010000, Astana
Phone: + 7 (7172) 105, 38-33-33

Balkhash Train Station
Balkhash City, Karagandy Province
Phone: +7 (71036) 6 55 33, 6 26 53, 6 26 24

Beyneu Train Station
Beyneu, Mangystau Province

Embi Train Station

Embi, Aktobe Province

Ganyushkino Train Station

Kurmangazy District, Atyrau Province

Kostanay Train Station

7, Perronnaya Str., 110003, Kostanay

Phone: + 7 (7142) 31-36-00, 31-36-08

Petropavlovsk Train Station

1, Koshukova, 150000, Petropavlovsk

Phone: + 7 (7152) 35-22-53, 35-22-00

Pavlodar Train Station

1, Privokzalnaya Ploshchad, 140000, Pavlodar

Phone: + 7 (7182) 105, 37-23-33, 37-21-44

Semey Train Station

1, Privokzalnaya Square, 071401, Semey

Phone: + 7 (7222) 98-32-32

Shymkent Train Station
Anarov Str., 160000, Shymkent
Phone: +7 7252 952 120

Taldykorgan Train Station
1, Vokzalnaya, 040000, Taldykorgan
Phone: +7 7282 272 882

Taraz Train Station
1, Privokzalnaya Str., 080001, Taraz
Phone: +7 (7262) 461 444

Uralsk Train Station
1/1, Chapaev Square, 090000, Uralsk
Phone: +7 7112 970 644, 516 647

Turan Express Private Railway Operator

Turan Express is a private passenger railway operator in Kazakhstan. Currently the provide transportation on the routes: Astana-Almaty, Almaty-Dostyk and Almaty-

Altynkol. In 2014 they are planning for launching high-speed trains along the route Astana - Kyzylorda, Almaty - Aktobe, Almaty-Protection, Astana - Protection and Almaty - Tashkent.

Train Stations in Kyrgyzstan

The Kyrgyz railroad network has one line: the north line - between Bishek and Balykchy. The south line - from Andijon, in Uzbekistan, to Osh and Jalal-Abad in Kyrgyzstan, was closed in 2010, after the revolution. The north line offers beautiful sceneries, the train carrying passengers through a mountain pass. The ride ends right at the shores of Issyk-kul Lake. You should check before planning a trip on this route because the trains operate only during summer.

The main routes are:

Bishek - Tashkent - Samarkand

Moscow - Bishek

Bishkek - Balykchy (Issyk-kul Lake)

Bishek Train Station

1 Erkindik Ave, Bishkek 720040, Kyrgyzstan

Balykchy Train Station
Balykchy, Kyrgyzstan

Train Stations in Laos

Thanaleng Train Station

Dongphosy village, Hadxayfong district, Vientiane Prefecture, Laos

Train Stations in Malaysia
Perlis

Arau Train Station

Stesen Keretapi Arau, Jalan Stesyen, 02600, Arau, Perlis

Phone: 04 986 1225

Padang Besar Train Station

Stesen Keretapi Padang Besar, Komplek KTM, Jalan Besar, 02100 Padang Besar, Perlis

Phone: 04 949 0231

Kedah

Alor Setar Train Station

Jalan Stesyen, 5000, Alor Setar, Kedah

Phone: 04 733 5022

Anak Bukit Train Station

Anak Bukit, Kedah

Phone: 04 714 3328

Bedong Train Station
Kedah
Phone: 04 458 9702

Gurun Train Station
Stesen Sementara KTMB, Kampung Pulau
Cengal, 08300 Gurun, Kedah, Malaysia
Phone: 04 468 6443

Junun Train Station
Kedah
Phone: 04 759 0504

Kodiang Train Station
Kodiang, Kedah
Phone: 04 925 7135

Sungai Petani Train Station

LLN5049, Stesyen Ktm, Jln Ibrahim, 08000, Sungai Petani, Kedah
Phone: 04 421 2604

Tunjang Train Station
Tunjang, Kedah
Phone: 04 929 2293

Penang

Bukit Mertajam Train Station
Stesen Keretapi Bukit Mertajam, 14000 Bukit Mertajam, Pulau Pinang, Malaysia
Phone: 04 539 2660

Bukit Tengah Train Station
Bukit Tengah, Pulau Pinang

Butterworth Train Station
Stesen Keretapi Butterworth, Jalan Bagan Dalam, 12000 Butterworth, Pulau Pinang, Malaysia

Phone: 04 331 2796

Penanti Train Station
Pulau Pinang
Phone: 04 522 4286

Pinang Tunggal Train Station
Pinang Tunggal, Pulau Pinang

Simpang Ampat Train Station
Simpang Ampat, Pulau Pinang

Tasik Gelugor Train Station
Tasik Gelugor, Pulau Pinang

Perak

Bagan Serai Train Station
Perak
Phone: 05 721 5284

Batu Gajah Train Station
Batu Gajah

Phone: 05 366 6601, 05 366 6616

Behrang Train Station
Perak
Phone: 05 454 2719, 05 453 0189

Bukit Merah Train Station
Perak
Phone: 05 721 3701

Chemor Train Station
Perak
Phone: 05 201 1268

Ipoh Train Station
Stesen Keretapi Ipoh, Jalan Panglima Bukit Gantang Wahab, 31000 Ipoh, Perak, Malaysia
Phone: 05 254 0481 / 05 243 9832

Kampar Train Station
Stesen Keretapi Kampar, Jalan Stesen, 31900 Kampar, Perak, Malaysia

Phone: 05 465 1489

Kamunting Train Station
Perak
Phone: 05 891 6672

Kota Bharu Train Station
Perak
Phone: 05 359 6311

Kuala Kangsar Train Station
Stesen Keretapi Kuala Kangsar, Jalan Sultan Idris, 33000 Kuala Kangsar, Perak, Malaysia
Phone: 05 776 1094

Lahat Train Station
Perak
Phone: 05 321 4785

Nibong Tebal Train Station
Pulau Pinang
Phone: 04 593 1308

Padang Rengas Train Station

Perak

Phone: 05 758 4206

Parit Buntar Train Station

Stesen Keretapi Parit Buntar, Parit Buntar, Perak, Malaysia

Phone: 05 716 1004

Pondok Tanjung Train Station

Perak

Phone: 05 883 8828

Salak Utara Train Station

Perak

Phone: 05 757 8910

Slim River Train Station

Stesen Keretapi Slim River, Jalan Stesen, 35800 Slim River, Perak, Malaysia

Phone: 05 452 7439

Sungai Siput Train Station

Stesen Keretapi Sungai Siput, 31100 Sungai Siput Utara, Perak, Malaysia
Phone: 05 598 1244

Sungkai Train Station

Stesen Keretapi Sungkai, 35600 Sungkai, Perak, Malaysia
Phone: 05 438 6132

Taiping Train Station

Stesen Keretapi Taiping, Taiping, Perak
Phone: 05 807 5584 / 05 807 2591

Tanjung Malim Train Station

Stesen Keretapi Tanjung Malim, Jalan Stesyen, 35900 Tanjung Malim, Perak, Malaysia
Phone: 05 450 1203

Tanjung Rambutan Train Station

Stesen Keretapi Tanjung Rambutan, 104/4, Jalan Stesyen, 31250 Tanjung Rambutan, Perak, Malaysia
Phone: 05 533 1237

Tapah Road Train Station

Stesen Keretapi Tapah Road, Dalam Kawasan Stesyen Keretapi, 35400 Tapah Road, Perak, Malaysia
Phone: 05 406 1236

Tasik Train Station

Perak
Phone: 05 547 1055

Selangor

Bangi Train Station

Selangor
Phone: 03 8925 6218

Batang Kali Train Station

Selangor

Phone: 03 6057 1790 / 03 6057 1792

Kajang Train Station

Selangor

Phone: 03 8733 1159

Kuala Kubu Bharu Train Station

Stesen Keretapi Kuala Kubu Bharu, Kuala
Kubu Bharu, Selangor, Malaysia

Phone: 03 6047 7925

Kuang Train Station

Selangor

Phone: 03 6037 1077

Rasa Train Station

Selangor

Phone: 03 6057 1814

Rawang Train Station

Stesen Keretapi Rawang, 41300 Rawang, Selangor, Malaysia
Phone: 03 6093 4584

Serendah Train Station
Selangor
Phone: 03 6081 2275

Shah Alam Train Station
Selangor
Phone: 03 5126 1951

Subang Jaya Train Station
Selangor
Phone: 03 5634 1671

Sungai Buloh Train Station
Stesen Keretapi Sungai Buloh, Lot 3, Jalan Kuala Selangor, 47000 Sungai Buloh, Selangor, Malaysia
Phone: 03 6156 1930

Kuala Lumpur

Angkasapuri Train Station

Perhentian KTMB Angkasapuri, Jalan Pantai Dalam, 59200, Kerinchi, Kuala Lumpur

Batu Caves Train Station

Batu Caves, Kuala Lumpur

Batu Kantonmen Train Station

Batu Kantonmen, Kuala Lumpur

Kampung Batu Train Station

Kampung Batu, Kuala Lumpur

Kepong Train Station

Selangor
Phone: 03 2263 1081

Kepong Sentral Train Station

Kepong, Selangor
Phone: 03 2263 1088

KL Sentral

Kuala Lumpur

Phone: 03 2273 1415

Kuala Lumpur Train Station

Stesen KTMB Kuala Lumpur, Jalan Hishamuddin, Kuala Lumpur, Malaysia

Phone: 03 2263 1363

MidValley Train Station

Kuala Lumpur

Phone: 03 2263 1088

Salak Selatan Train Station

Kuala Lumpur

Phone: 03 7980 7823

Sentul Train Station

Jalan Perhentian, Sentul, Kuala Lumpur

Phone: 03 4041 7620

Negeri Sembilan

Air Kuning Selatan Train Station
Negeri Sembilan
Phone: 06 447 8417

Bahau Train Station
Negeri Sembilan
Phone: 06 454 1237

Batang Benar Train Station
Negeri Sembilan
Phone: 06 799 1248

Rembau Train Station
Negeri Sembilan
Phone: 06 685 3126

Seremban Train Station
Negeri Sembilan
Phone: 06 762 2141

Gemas Train Station
Negeri Sembilan
Phone: 07 948 1026

Malacca

Batang Melaka Train Station
Melaka
Phone: 06 446 1310

Tampin / Pulau Sebang Train Station
Melaka
Phone: 06 441 1034

Johore

Batu Anam Train Station
Johor
Phone: 07 949 7727

Bekok Train Station
Stesen Keretapi Bekok, Jalan Station, 86500 Bekok, Johor Darul Takzim, Malaysia
Phone: 07 922 1217

Genuang Train Station
Johor
Phone: 07 943 7800

JB Sentral Train Station
Johore
Phone: 07 223 3040, 07 223 4727

Kempas Baru Train Station
Stesen Keretapi Kempas Baru, Kempas Baru, 81200 Johor Bahru, Johor Darul Takzim
Phone: 07 236 3757

Kluang Train Station
Stesen Keretapi Kluang, Jalan Station, 86000 Kluang, Johor Darul Takzim
Phone: 07 772 2039

Kulai Train Station
Stesen Keretapi Kulai, Jalan Raya, 81000 Kulai, Johor Darul Takzim, Malaysia
Phone: 07 663 1507

Layang-layang Train Station
Johor
Phone: 07 752 7199

Mengkibol Train Station
Johor
Phone: 07 772 3344

Paloh Train Station
Stesen Keretapi Paloh, No. 39 Jalan Station, 86600 Paloh, Johor Darul Takzim, Malaysia
Phone: 07 781 1268

Rengam Train Station
Johor
Phone: 07 753 5120

Segamat Train Station
Stesen Keretapi Segamat, Jalan Station, 85000 Segamat, Johor Darul Takzim, Malaysia

Phone: 07 935 1487, 07 931 1021

Tenang Train Station

Tenang, 85000, Segamat, Johor

Phone: 07 927 0705

Labis Train Station

Stesen Keretapi Labis, 85300 Labis, Johor
Darul Takzim, Malaysia

Phone: 07 925 1134

Pahang

Jerantut Train Station

Stesen Keretapi Jerantut, No. 687, Jalan
Stesen, Bandar Baru, 27000 Jerantut,
Pahang, Malaysia

Phone: 09 266 2219

Kemayan Train Station

Pahang

Phone: 09 240 9236

Kuala Krau Train Station

Stesen Keretapi Kuala Krau, Jalan Kampung Paya Luas, 28050 Kuala Krau, Pahang, Malaysia
Phone: 09 312 7031, 09 286 1237

Kuala Lipis Train Station

Stesen Keretapi Kuala Lipis, Jalan Pekeliling, 27200 Kuala Lipis, Pahang, Malaysia
Phone: 09 312 1522

Mentakab Train Station

Stesen Keretapi Mentakab, Jalan Stesyen, 28400 Mentakab, Pahang, Malaysia
Phone: 09 277 1002

Sultan Haji Ahmad Shah Airport

Kuantan, Pahang, Malaysia

Triang Train Station

Stesen Keretapi Triang, 28300 Triang, Pahang, Malaysia

Phone: 09 255 7749

Kelantan

Dabong Train Station

Stesen Keretapi Dabong, 18200 Dabong, Kelantan, Malaysia
Phone: 09 965 7371

Gua Musang Train Station

Stesen Keretapi Gua Musang, 18300 Gua Musang, Kelantan, Malaysia
Phone: 09 312 7019, 09 912 1226

Pasir Mas Train Station

Stesen Keretapi Pasir Mas, Jalan Besar, 17000 Pasir Mas, Kelantan, Malaysia
Phone: 09 790 9025

Tanah Merah Train Station

Stesen Keretapi Tanah Merah, Jalan Machang, 17500 Machang, Kelantan, Malaysia
Phone: 09 955 6025

Tumpat Train Station
Stesen Keretapi Tumpat, Jalan Besar, 16200 Tumpat, Kelantan, Malaysia
Phone: 09 725 7232/7242

Wakaf Bahru Train Station
Stesen Keretapi Wakaf Bahru, No. 33, Jalan Hadapan Stesen Keretapi, 16250 Wakaf Baru, Kelantan, Malaysia
Phone: 09 7196986

Train Stations in Mongolia

The most important route, the Trans-Mongolian route, is part of the international line between Russia and China also called the Trans Siberian railway that starts in Russia and crosses Mongolia to arrive in Beijing, China. This is the longest continuous rail line on Earth so expect to find the train pretty crowded. It is also advisable to book your tickets well in advance if you want to book a seat in the Trans Siberian train.

The main station from where you can buy tickets either for Moscow or Beijing is Ulaanbaatar.

Ulaanbaatar Train Station
Khoroo 1, Ulaanbaatar
Phone (foreigner booking office): 24133, inquiries 243 848; Room 212; 8am-7pm

Darkhan Train Station

Darkhan

Phone (ticket office): 42301

Erlian Train Station

No.28, Yingbin Road, Erenhot City, Xilin Gol League

Phone: 0479-2229223

Sainshand Train Station

Dornogovi province

Sükhbaatar Train Station

Selenge

Phone: 976 1362 40124

Zuunkharaa Train Station

Mandal sum District of Selenge Province

Train Stations in Nepal

Nepal has only one rail line that crosses 32 km. The line connects Janakpur, in Nepal, and Jainagar, in India.

Bijalpura Train Station

Bijalpura Town, Railway Station Area, Southern Nepal (close to the border with India)

Janakpur Train Station

Janakpur, Central Region, Dhanusa District, Janakpur Zone

Khajuri Train Station

Khajuri Chanha, Dhanusa District, Janakpur Zone of south-eastern Nepal

Mahinathpur Train Station

Mahinathpur-Tinkauriya Chowk

Train Stations in North Korea

Tourists can visit North Korea only as part of organized tours planned by travel agencies. The only transport hub for entering North Korea is Beijing which offers connections with Pyongyang, the capital of North Korea. Although there is the possibility for tourists to enter from Russia, nowadays this is practically impossible because tourists are often required to pick up their visas in Beijing.

Anbyon Train Station

Anbyon County, Kangwon province

Chimchon Train Station

Hwangju County, North Hwanghae Province

Chongbang Train Station

Sariwon, North Hwanghae Province

Chongchongang Train Station

Pakchon County, North Pyongan

Chunghwa Train station
Chunghwa County, North Hwanghae Province

Hanpo Train Station
Hanpo-ri, Pyongsan County, North Hwanghae Province

Hukkyo Train Station
Hwangju County, North Hwanghae Province

Hungsu Train Station
Hwanghae-bukto, North Hwanghae Province

Hwangju Train Station
Hwangju, North Hwanghae Province

Kaepung Train Station
Kaepung-gun, North Hwanghae province

Kalli Train Station

Hyongjesan-guyok, Pyongyang

Kowon Train Station
Kowon, South Hamgyong Province

Kwaksan Train Station
Kwaksan County, North Pyongan Province

Mundok Train Station
Mundok County, South Pyongan Province

Opa Train Station
Pyongwon County, South Pyongan Province

Panmun Train Station
Kaesŏng Industrial Region

Pongdong Train Station
Pongsan County, North Hwanghae Province

Pongsan Train Station

Pongsan County, North Hwanghae Province

Pyongsan Train Station
Pyongsan County, North Hwanghae Province

Pyongyang Train Station
Pyongyang

Sariwon Chongnyon Train Station
Sariwon, North Hwanghae Province

Sepo Chongnyon Train Station
Sepo County, Kangwon province

Sinmak Train Station
North Hwanghae Province

Sinuiju Train Station
Sinuiju, North Pyongan Province

Sohung Train Station

North Hwanghae Province

Sonchon Train Station
Sonchon County, North Pyongan

Sonha Train Station
Kaesong, North Hwanghae Province

Sukchon Train Station
Sukchon County, South Pyongan Province

Taebaeksansong Train Station
Pyongsan County, North Hwanghae Province

Tongrim Train Station
Tongrim County, North Pyongan Province

Unjon Train Station
Unjon County, North Pyongan Province

Wonsan Train Station

AH6, Wonsan, Kangwon Province

Train Stations in Pakistan
Punjab

Abdul-Hakim Train Station
Khanewal District, Punjab, Pakistan

Arifwala Train Station
Arifwala, Punjab, Pakistan

Attock Train Station
Pedestrian crossing, Attock, Pakistan

Bhakkar Train Station
Bhakkar, Punnjab, Pakistan

Bahawalpur Train Station
Bahawalpur, Punjab, Pakistan

Bhalwal Train Station
Sargodha Bhalwal Rd., Bhalwal, Punjab

Burewala Train Station

Burewala, Punjab, Pakistan

Chiniot Train Station
Railway Station Rd, Chiniot, Pakistan

Faisalabad Train Station
Station Rd, Faisalabad 54000, Pakistan

Farooq Abad Train Station
Sargodha Rd, Sheikhupura District, Punjab,
Pakistan

Gujar Khan Train Station
Gujar Khan, Rawalpindi District, Punjab,
Pakistan

Gujranwala Train Station
Civil Lines, Gujranwala 52250, Pakistan

Gujrat Train Station
Gujrat-50700, Punjab

Jauharabad Train Station

Qaidabad Rd, Jauharabad, Pakistan

Jhang Train Station
Jhang Sadar, Jhang, Pakistan

Kasur Train Station
Railway Rd (Crossing Circular Rd), Kas$^{\bar{u}}$r, Punjab

Khanewal Junction Train Station
Khanewal, Pakistan

Khushab Train Station
Railway Rd, Khushab, Punjab

Kot Radha kishan Train Station
Kot Radha Kishan, Pakistan

Lalamusa Junction Train Station
Karimpura, Lalamusa, Pakistan

Lahore Junction Train Station
G.T. Road, Lahore, Punjab, Pakistan

Mailsi Train Station
Railway Rd, Mailsi, Pakistan

Malakwal Junction Train Station
Railway Rd, Malakw$^{\bar{a}}$l, Pakistan

Multan Cantonment Train Station
Multan, Pakistan

Multan City Train Station
Setal Mari, Multan, Pakistan

Muzaffarabad Train Station, Multan
Sher Shah Rd, Muzaffarabad, Punjab

Muzaffargarh Train Station
Railway Rd, Muzaffargarh, Pakistan

Okara Train Station
Allama Iqbal Rd, Ok$^{\bar{a}}$ra, Pakistan

Pakpattan Train Station

Railway Rd, Pākpattan, Pakistan

Rahim Yar Khan Train Station
Railway Rd, Rahim Yar Khan, Pakistan

Raiwind Junction Train Station
Raiwind Rd, Raiwind, Punjab

Rao Khan Wala Train Station
Rao Khan Wala, Punjab

Rawalpindi Train Station
Rawalpindi, Punjab
Phone: 051-9270395

Sargodha Junction Train Station
Railway Rd, Sargodha, Pakistan

Sheikhupura Junction Train Station
Malik Anwar Rd, Civil Lines, Sheikhupura,
Pakistan

Sher Shah Junction Train Station, Multan

Sher Shah Rd, Multan, Pakistan

Sialkot Junction Train Station

Railway Rd, Si$^{\bar{a}}$lkot, Pakistan

Vehari Train Station

Station Rd, Veh$^{\bar{a}}$ri, Pakistan

Wagah Train Station

Wagah, Lahore District, Pakistan

Wazirabad Junction Train Station

Station Rd, Wazirabad, Punjab, Pakistan

Sindh

Dadu Train Station

Railway Station Rd, Dadu, Sindh, Pakistan

Drigh Road Train Station

Drigh Rd, Karachi, Pakistan

Hyderabad Junction Train Station

Station Rd, Hyderabad, Sindh

Jacobabad Train Station

Station Rd, Jacobabad, Sindh

Karachi City Train Station

Station Street, Karachi City, Sindh

Karachi Cantonment Train Station

Dr. Daud Pota Road, Karachi, Sindh

Khairpur Train Station

Station Rd, Khairpur, Sindh

Kotri Junction Train Station

Kotri Station Rd, Kotri, Sindh

Landhi Train Station

Station Rd, Karachi, Sindh

Larkana Train Station

Station Rd, Larkana, Sindh

Mehrabpur Junction Train Station
Station Rd, Mahrabpur, Pakistan

Setharja (City)
Station Rd, Khairpur District, Sindh

Mirpur Khas Train Station
Railway Quarters Rd, Mīrpur Khās, Sindh

Nawabshah Train Station
Station Rd, Nawabshah, Sindh

Sehwan Train Station
Indus Hwy, Sehwān, Sindh

Rohri Junction Train Station
Rohri, Pakistan

Sukkur Train Station
Station Rd, Sukkur, Sindh

Tando Adam Train Station

Tando $\bar{\text{A}}$dam, Sindh

Zero Point Train Station

Zero Point, Mirpur Khas District, Sindh

Bandhi Train Station

Bandhi, Shaheed Benazir Abad District, Sindh

Daur Train Station

Bandhi Rd, Daur, Sindh

Balochistan

Chaman Train Station

Chaman Bypass Rd, Chaman, Balochistan

Dalbandin Train Station

Dalbandin, Balochistan

Mach Train Station

Mach, Balochistan

Quetta Train Station

Joint Rd, Quetta, Balochistan

Spezand Junction Train Station

Spezand, Balochistan

Sibi Train Station

Station Rd, Sibi, Balochistan

Khyber Pakhtunkhwa

Havelian Train Station

Railway Rd, Havelian, Khyber Pakhtunkhwa

Nowshehra Train Station

Station Rd, Nowshera, Khyber Pakhtunkhwa

Peshawar Cantonment Train Station

Railway Rd, Peshawar, Khyber Pakhtunkhwa

Train Stations in Philippines

The rail lines in Philippines are under the administration of Philippine National Railways. PNR operates in Manila metropolitan area and the provinces of Laguna, Quezon, Camarines Sur (Naga City) and Albay.

Starting with 2011, PNR resumed daily train rides between Manila and Naga City operated by Bicol Express, which were discounted following the typhoon damage. This train is quite comfortable and safe. Also, from 2012, PNR introduced the Mayon Limited trains that operate beyond Naga to Ligao.

At the moment of writing this travel guide, those rail lines were once again closed following the hurricane of 2012.

Agdangan Train Station

Agdangan, Philippines

Alabang Train Station
T. Molina Street, Alabang, Muntinlupa
1781

Bicutan Train Station
General Santos Avenue, San Martin de
Porres, Parañaque City

Binan Train Station
General Malvar Street, San Vicente, Biñan
City, Laguna

Blumentritt Train Station
Old Antipolo Street, Rizal Avenue and
Leonor Rivera Street, Sta. Cruz, Manila

Buendia Train Station
South Luzon Expressway cor. Gil Puyat
Avenue, Pio del Pilar, Makati City

Calamba Train Station

Rizal Street, Barangay 1, Calamba City, Laguna

EDSA Train Station

South Luzon Expressway, Magallanes, Makati

Espana Train Station

Antipolo St, Sampaloc, Manila

FTI Train Station

East Service Road cor. FTI Rd., Western Bicutan, Taguig City

Gumaca Train Station

Gumaca, Quezon

Hondagua Train Station

Hondagua, Lopez

Laong Laan Train Station

Laong Laan Street, Sampaloc, Manila

Libmanan Train Station

Libmanan, near Colegio Del Santissimo Rosario

Ligao Train Station

Barangay Tinago, Ligao City, Albay

Lucena Train Station

Barangay 10, South City Proper, Lucena City, Quezon

Naga Train Station

PNR Road, Tabuco, Naga City

Nichols Train Station

East Service Road, Western Bicutan, Taguig City

Paco Train Station

Quirino Avenue cor. Pedro Gil Street, Paco, Manila

Pamplona Train Station

Pamplona, Philippines

Pandacan Train Station

Padre Zamora Street, Pandacan, Manila

Pasay Road Train Station

Estacion Street, Pio del Pilar, Makati City

Polangui Train Station

Polangui, Province of Albay

Ragay Train Station

Ragay, Liboro, Philippines

San Andres Train Station

South Luzon Expressway cor. San Andres St., San Andres, Manila

San Pablo Train Station

Barangay II, San Pablo City, Laguna

Santa Mesa Train Station

Ramon Magsaysay Boulevard and Teresa St., Santa Mesa, Manila

Sipocot Train Station

Rolando R. Andaya Hwy, Sipocot, Philippines

Sucat Train Station

Meralco Road, Sucat, Muntinlupa City

Tagkawayan Train Station

San Rafael St., Tagkawayan, Philippines

Tutuban Train Station

PNR Executive Building, Mayhaligue Street, Tondo, Manila

Vito Cruz Train Station

South Luzon Expressway cor. Pablo Ocampo Street Ext., San Andres, Manila

Train Stations in Saudi Arabia

Dammam Train Station
Fatema Al Zahra St, Abdullah Fuad, Dammam

Haradh Train Station
Al-Hasa, Saudi Arabia
Phone: 03-5828286

Hofuf Train Station
King Fahd road, near to Al-Ahsa Hospital

Makkah Train Station
Al Rasaifah, Ar Rusayfah, Mecca 24232, Saudi Arabia

Riyadh Train Station
Hasan Al Shawri St., Riyadh 12844, Saudi Arabia

Abqaiq Station Train Station

Al-Muntazah St., near Saudi Aramco's
main gate

Train Stations in Singapore

Bukit Timah Train Station

5 King Albert Park, Singapore 598287

Tanjong Pagar Train Station

30 Keppel Road, Singapore 089059

Train Stations in South Korea
Busan

Bujeon Train Station

Bujeon-dong, Busanjin District, Busan

Busan Train Station

Choryang-dong, Dong District, Busan, South Korea

Busanjin Train Station

Jwacheon-dong, Dong District, Busan, South Korea

Gupo Train Station

Gupo-dong, Buk District, Busan, South Korea

Hwamyeong Train Station

Hwamyeong-dong, Buk District, Busan

Sasang Train Station

Gwaebeop-dong, Sasang District, Busan

North Chungcheong Province

Bongyang Train Station
Jangpyeong-ri, Bongyang-eup, Jecheon, North Chungcheong

Cheonan-Asan Train Station
419-1 Jangjaeri, Baebang-eup, Asan-si, Chungcheongnam-do

Chupungnyeong Train Station
336-1 Chupungnyeong-ri, Chupungnyeong-myeon, Yeongdong-gun, Chungcheongbuk-do, South Korea

Gakgye Train Station
Gakgye-ri, Simcheon-myeon, Yeongdong-gun, Chungcheongbuk-do, South Korea

Hwanggan Train Station

42 Masan-ri, Hwanggan-myeon, Yeongdong-gun, Chungcheongbuk-do, South Korea

Iwon Train Station

23 Gangcheong-ri, Iwon-myeon, Okcheon-gun, Chungcheongbuk-do, South Korea

Jecheon Train Station

Yeongcheon-dong, Jecheon, North Chungcheong, South Korea

Jitan Train Station

28 Jitan-ri, Iwon-myeon, Okcheon-gun, Chungcheongbuk-do, South Korea

Okcheon Train Station

112-1 Geumgu-ri, Okcheon-eup, Okcheon-gun, Chungcheongbuk-do, South Korea

Osong Train Station

Bongsan-ri, Osong-eup, Cheongwon-gun, North Chungcheong, South Korea

Simcheon Train Station

318-6 Simcheon-ri, Simcheon-myeon, Yeongdong-gun, Chungcheongbuk-do, South Korea

Sinchang Train Station

346-7 Haengmongni, Sinchang-myeon, Asan-si, Chungcheongnam-do

Yeongdong Train Station

205 Gyesan-ri, Yeongdong-eup, Yeongdong-gun, Chungcheongbuk-do, South Korea

South Chungcheong Province

Cheonan Train Station

57-1 Daeheung-dong, 239 Daeheung-ro, Dongnam-gu, Cheonan-si, Chungcheongnam-do

Gyeryong Train Station
Dugye-ri, Duma-myeon, Gyeryong, South Chungcheong, South Korea

Namgongju Train Station
Lin-myeon, Gongju, South Chungcheong, South Korea

Nonsan Train Station
33 Chwiam-dong, Nonsan-si, Chungcheongnam-do, South Korea

Onyangoncheon Train Station
69-10 Oncheon-dong, Asan-si, Chungcheongnam-do, South Korea

Seonghwan Train Station
449-128 Seonghwanni, 237-5 Seonghwan 1-ro, Seonghwan-eup, Seobuk-gu, Cheonan-si, Chungcheongnam-do

Daegu

Daegu Train Station

302-155 Chilseong 1(il)-ga, Buk-gu, Daegu, South Korea

Dongdaegu Train Station

294 Sinam-dong, Dong District, Daegu

Gacheon Train Station

363 Gacheon-dong, Suseong-gu, Daegu, South Korea

Gomo Train Station

384-1 Gomo-dong, Suseong-gu, Daegu, South Korea

Daejeon

Daejeon Train Station

1 Jeong-dong, Dong-gu, Daejeon, South Korea

Daejeonjochajang Train Station

426 Eupnae-dong, Daedeok-gu, Daejeon, South Korea

Hoedeok Train Station
134 Sindae-dong, Daedeok-gu, Daejeon, South Korea

Secheon Train Station
Chu-dong, Dong-gu, Daejeon, South Korea

Seodaejeon Train Station
74 Yucheon-dong, Jung-gu, Daejeon, South Korea

Sintanjin Train Station
146-1 Sintanjin-dong, Daedeok-gu, Daejeon, South Korea

Gangwon

Chuncheon Train Station
190 Geunhwa-dong, Chuncheon-si, Gangwon-do, South Korea

Donghae Train Station

Songjeong-dong, Donghae, Gangwon, South Korea

Gangchon Train Station

88-2 Gangchon-ri, Namsan-myeon, Chuncheon-si, Gangwon-do, South Korea

Gangneung Train Station

Gyo-dong, Gangneung, Gangwon, South Korea

Jeongseon Train Station

428 Aesan-ri, Jeongseon-eup, Jeongseon-gun, Gangwon-do, South Korea

Namchuncheon Train Station

375-8 Toegye-dong, 2 Namchunno, Chuncheon-si, Gangwon-do

Samcheok Train Station

Sajik-dong, Samcheok, Gangwon, South Korea

Taebaek Train Station
Hwangji-dong, Taebaek, Gangwon, South Korea

Wonju Train Station
Hakseong-dong, Wonju, Gangwon, South Korea

Gwangju

Dongsongjeong Train Station
Doho-dong, Gwangsan-gu, Gwangju, South Korea

Gwangju Songjeong Train Station
1003-1 Songjeong-dong, Gwangsan-gu, Gwangju, South Korea

Gwangju Train Station

611 Jungheung-dong, Buk-gu, Gwangju, South Korea

Hyocheon Train Station

482-6 Songha-dong, Nam-gu, Gwangju, South Korea

Seogwangju Train Station

186-5 Maewol-dong, Seo-gu, Gwangju, South Korea

Gyeonggi

Anyang Train Station

88-1 Anyang 1-dong, 232 Mananno, Manan-gu, Anyang-si, Gyeonggi-do

Cheongpyeong Train Station

175 Cheongpyeongni, 38-163 Jamgokjageunno, Cheongpyeong-myeon, Gapyeong-gun, Gyeonggi-do

Choseong-ri Train Station

440 Choseong-ri, Cheongsan-myeon, Yeoncheon-gun, Gyeonggi-do

Daegwang-ri Train Station

235 Dosin-ri, Sinseo-myeon, Yeoncheon-gun, Gyeonggi-do

Deokso Train Station

590-17 Deokso-ri, Wabu-eup, Namyangju-si, Gyeonggi-do

Dongducheon Train Station

688 Saengyeon-dong, Dongducheon-si, Gyeonggi-do

Dorasan Train Station

Nosang-ri, Jangdan-myeon, Paju, Gyeonggi Province

Gapyeong Train Station

603-2 Daljeon-ri, 13-42, Munhwaro, Gapyeong-eup, Gapyeong-gun, Gyeonggi-do

Gwangmyeong Train Station

267-8 Iljik-dong, 21 Gwangmyeongyeongno, Gwangmyeong-si, Gyeonggi-do

Haengsin Train Station

802 Haengsin 2-dong, Deogyang-gu, Goyang, Gyeonggi-do

Hantangang Train Station

Jeongok-ri, Jeongok-eup, Yeoncheon-gun, Gyeonggi-do

Imjingang Train Station

1253-3 Majeong-ri, Munsan-eup, Paju-si, Gyeonggi-do

Jeongok Train Station

333-10 Jeongok-ri, Jeongok-eup, Yeoncheon-gun, Gyeonggi-do

Maseok Train Station
292 Maseokwoo-ri, Hwado-eup, Namyangju-si, Gyeonggi-do

Munsan Train Station
17 Munsan-ri, Munsan-eup, Paju-si, Gyeonggi-do

Osan Train Station
603-116 Osan-dong, 59 Yeokgwangjangno, Osan-si, Gyeonggi-do

Pyeongnae-Hopyeong Train Station
156 Pyeongnae-dong, Namyangju-si, Gyeonggi-do

Pyeongtaek Train Station
185-1 Pyeongtaek-dong, 51 Pyeongtaengno, Pyeongtaek-si, Gyeonggi-do

Samsan Train Station

Samsan-ri, Yangdong-myeon, Yangpyeong-gun, Gyeonggi-do

Sareung Train Station

590-2 Saneung-ri, 72-8, Jingeonuhoero, Jingeon-eup, Namyangju-si, Gyeonggi-do

Seojeong-ri Train Station

427-1 Seojeong-dong, 51 Tanhyeonno, Pyeongtaek-si, Gyeonggi-do

Sinmang-ri Train Station

100 Sang-ri, Yeoncheon-eup, Yeoncheon-gun, Gyeonggi-do

Sintan-ri Train Station

172 Daegwang-ri, Sinseo-myeon, Yeoncheon-gun, Gyeonggi-do

Soyosan Train Station

126-3   Sangbongam-dong,   2925
Pyeonghwaro, Dongducheon-si, Gyeonggi-
do

Suwon Train Station
18 Maesanro 1-ga, 924 Deogyeongdaero,
Paldal-gu, Suwon-si, Gyeonggi-do

Toegyewon Train Station
218-142   Toegyewon-ri,   545
Gyeongchunbungno,   Toegyewon-myeon,
Namyangju-si, Gyeonggi-do

Uijeongbu Train Station
168-54   Uijeongbu   2-dong,   525
Pyeonghwaro, Uijeongbu-si, Gyeonggi-do

Uncheon Train Station
Uncheon-ri,   Munsan-eup,   Paju-si,
Gyeonggi-do

Yangpyeong (Jungang Line)Train Station

137 Yanggeunni, 30, Yeokjeongil, Yangpyeong-eup, Yangpyeong-gun, Gyeonggi-do

Yeoncheon Train Station

34 Chatan-ri, Yeoncheon-eup, Yeoncheon-gun, Gyeonggi-do

Yongmun Train Station

737 Damunni, 18 Yongmun-yeokgil, Yongmun-myeon, Yangpyeong-gun, Gyeonggi-do

North Gyeongsang Province

Andong Train Station

224 Unheung-dong, Andong-si, Gyeongsangbuk-do

Apo Train Station

Gugsa-ri, Apo-eup, Gimcheon-si, Gyeongsangbuk-do

Baegwon Train Station

Wonheung-ri, Sabeol-myeon, Sangju-si, Gyeongsangbuk-do

Bonghwa Train Station

Haejeo-ri, Bonghwa-eup, Bonghwa, North Gyeongsang

Cheongdo Train Station

969-2 Gosu-ri, Cheongdo-eup, Cheongdo-gun, Gyeongsangbuk-do

Cheongni Train Station

Wonjang-ri, Cheongni-myeon, Sangju-si, Gyeongsangbuk-do

Daesin Train Station

782 Daesin-ri, Apo-eup, Gimcheon-si, Gyeongsangbuk-do

Eodeung Train Station

689 Dokyang-ri, Bomun-myeon, Yecheon-gun, Gyeongsangbuk-do

Gaepo Train Station
Pungjeong-ri, Gaepo-myeon, Yecheon, North Gyeongsang

Gimcheon Train Station
264-1 Pyeonghwa-dong, Gimcheon-si, Gyeongsangbuk-do

Gimcheon–Gumi Train Station
790 Oksan-ri, Nam-myeon, Gimcheon-si, Gyeongsangbuk-do

Gumi Train Station
Wonpyeong-dong, Gumi, North Gyeongsang

Gyeongju Train Station
Seongdong-dong, Gyeongju, North Gyeongsang

Gyeongsan Train Station

84 Sajeong-dong, Gyeongsan-si, Gyeongsangbuk-do

Hamchang Train Station

166 Guhyang-ri, Hamchang-eup, Sangju-si, Gyeongsangbuk-do

Hwabon Train Station

Hwabon-ri, Sanseong-myeon, Gunwi, North Gyeongsang

Jeomchon Train Station

49 Jeomchon-dong, Mungyeong-si, Gyeongsangbuk-do

Jicheon Train Station

Yongsan-ri, Jicheon-myeon, Chilgok-gun, Gyeongsangbuk-do

Jikjisa Train Station

Daehang-myeon, Gimcheon-shi, Gyeongsangbuk-do

Jinyeong Train Station
131-1 Seolchang-ri, Jinyeong-eup, Gimhae-si, Gyeongsangnam-do

Munsu Train Station
Munsu, Munsuyeok, North Gyeongsang

Namseonghyeon Train Station
426-4 Daro-ri, Hwayang-eup, Cheongdo-gun, Gyeongsangbuk-do

Oksan Train Station
Sanhyeon-ri, Gongseong-myeon, Sangju-si, Gyeongsangbuk-do

Pohang Train Station
Daeheung-dong, Pohang, North Gyeongsang

Sagok Train Station

Sagok-dong, Gumi-si, Gyeongsangbuk-do

Samseong (Gyeongsan)Train Station
Samsung-ri, Namcheon-myeon, Gyeongsan-si, Gyeongsangbuk-do

Sangju Train Station
621 Seongdong-dong, Sangju-si, Gyeongsangbuk-do

Sinam Train Station
228 Sinam-ri, Bongsan-myeon, Gimcheon-si, Gyeongsangbuk-do

Sindong Train Station
506 Sin-ri, Jicheon-myeon, Chilgok-gun, Gyeongsangbuk-do

Singeo Train Station
Sindo-ri, Cheongdo-eup, Cheongdo-gun, Gyeongsangbuk-do

Singyeongju Train Station

1010 Hwacheon-ri, Geoncheon-eup, Gyeongju-si, Gyeongsangbuk-do

Uiseong Train Station
829 Hujuk-ri, Uiseong-eup Uiseong-gun, Gyeongsangbuk-do

Waegwan Train Station
230 Waegwan-ri, Waegwan-eup, Chilgok-gun, Gyeongsangbuk-do

Yangmok Train Station
147-1 Bokseong-ri, Yakmok-myeon, Chilgok-gun, Gyeongsangbuk-do

Yecheon Train Station
212-7 Noha-ri, Yecheon-eup, Yecheon-gun, Gyeongsangbuk-do

Yeongcheon Train Station
Wansan-dong, Yeongcheon, North Gyeongsang

Yeongju Train Station

349-1 Hyucheon-dong, Yeongju-si, Gyeongsangbuk-do

Yeonhwa Train Station

906 Yeonhwa-ri, Jicheon-myeon, Chilgok-gun, Gyeongsangbuk-do

Yonggung Train Station

336 Eupbu-ri, Yonggung-myeon, Yecheon-gun, Gyeongsangbuk-do

South Gyeongsang

Banseong Train Station

450 Changchon-ri, Ilbanseong-myeon, Jinju-si, Gyeongsangnam-do

Changwon Train Station

708-76 Dongjeong-dong, Uichang-gu, Gyeongsangnam-do

Changwonjungang Train Station

381 Sangnam-ro, Uichang-gu, Changwon-si

Dasolsa Train Station

474 Bonggye-ri, Gonmyeong-myeon, Sacheon-si, Gyeongsangnam-do

Deoksan Train Station

206 Yongjam-ri, Dong-eup, Uichang-gu, Gyeongsangnam-do

Gunbuk Train Station

254 Jungam-ri, Gunbuk-myeon, Haman-gun, Gyeongsangnam-do

Hadong Train Station

Bipa-ri, Hadong-eup, Hadong-gun, Gyeongsangnam-do

Hallimjeong Train Station

Jangbang-ri, Hallim-myeon, Gimhae-si, Gyeongsangnam-do

Haman Train Station

58-7 Malsan-ri, Gaya-eup, Haman-gun, Gyeongsangnam-do

Hoengcheon Train Station

Hoengcheon-ri, Hoengcheon-myeon, Hadong-gun, Gyeongsangnam-do

Jillye Train Station

684 Daman-ri, Jillye-myeon, Gimhae-si, Gyeongsangnam-do

Jinju Train Station

245 Gangnam-dong, Jinju-si, Gyeongsangnam-do

Jung-ri Train Station

445 Jung-ri, Naeseo-eup, Masanhoewon-gu, Gyeongsangnam-do

Masan Train Station

764-3 Hapseong-dong, Masanhoewon-gu, Gyeongsangnam-do

Miryang Train Station

662   Gagok-dong,   Miryang-si,
Gyeongsangnam-do

Mulgeum Train Station

372-3 Mulgeum-ri, Mulgeum-eup, Yangsan-si, Gyeongsangnam-do

Nakdonggang Train Station

Samrang-ri, Samnangjin-eup, Miryang-si,
Gyeongsangnam-do

Samnangjin Train Station

156-1 Songji-ri, Samnangjin-eup, Miryang-si, Gyeongsangnam-do

Wansa Train Station

120-14 Jeonggok-ri, Gonmyeong-myeon, Sacheon-si, Gyeongsangnam-do

Yangbo Train Station

Ubok-ri, Yangbo-myeon, Hadong-gun, Gyeongsangnam-do

North Jeolla Province

Gimje Train Station
Sinpung-dong, Gimje, North Jeolla

Iksan Train Station
1 Changin 1(il)-ga dong, Iksan-si, Jeollabuk-do

Jeongeup Train Station
343-1 Yeonji-dong, Jeongeup-si, Jeollabuk-do

South Jeolla Province

Beolgyo Train Station
890 Beolgyo-ri, Beolgyo-eup, Boseong-gun, Jeollanam-do

Boseong Train Station

928   Boseong-ri,   Boseong-eup,   Boseong-gun, Jeollanam-do

Deungnyang Train Station
909-1   Obong-ri,   Deungnyang-myeon, Boseong-gun, Jeollanam-do

Goryak Train Station
Hwanggeum-dong,   Gwangyang-si, Jeollanam-do

Guryong (Suncheon)Train Station
Guryong-ri,   Byeollyang-myeon,   Suncheon-si, Jeollanam-do

Gwanggok Train Station
Gwanggok-ri, Nodong-myeon, Boseong-gun, Jeollanam-do

Gwangyang Train Station
573-8   Dowol-ri,   Gwangyang-eup, Gwangyang-si, Jeollanam-do

Hwasun Train Station

507 Byeokra-ri, Hwasun-eup, Hwasun-gun, Jeollanam-do

Imseong-ri Train Station

759 Ogam-dong, Mokpo-si, Jeollanam-do

Iyang Train Station

Oryu-ri, Iyang-myeon, Hwasun-gun, Jeollanam-do

Jangseong Train Station

Yeongcheon-ri, Jangseong-eup, Jangseong, South Jeolla

Jinsang Train Station

Seomgeo-ri, Jinsang-myeon, Gwangyang-si, Jeollanam-do

Joseong Train Station

Joseong-ri, Joseong-myeon, Boseong-gun, Jeollanam-do

Mokpo Train Station
Honam-dong, Mokpo-si, Jeollanam-do

Myeongbong Train Station
Myeongbong-ri, Nodong-myeon, Boseong-gun, Jeollanam-do

Naju Train Station
Songwol-dong, Naju, South Jeolla

Nampyeong Train Station
Gwangchon-ri, Nampyeong-eup, Naju-si, Jeollanam-do

Neungju Train Station
230-2 Gwanyeong-ri, Neungju-myeon, Hwasun-gun, Jeollanam-do

Okgok Train Station

17 Singeum-ri, Okgok-myeon, Gwangyang-si, Jeollanam-do

Suncheon Train Station
139-22 Jogok-dong, Suncheon-si, Jeollanam-do

Wonchang Train Station
Dongsong-ri, Byeollyang-myeon, Suncheon-si, Jeollanam-do

Yedang Train Station
Yeodang-ri, Deungnyang-myeon, Boseong-gun, Jeollanam-do

Yeocheon Train Station
Yeocheon-dong, Yeosu, South Jeolla

Yeosu Expo Train Station
Deokchung-dong, Yeosu, South Jeolla

Sejong

Bugang Train Station

Bugang-ri, Buyong-myeon, Cheongwon-gun, Chungcheongbuk-do

Jeondong Train Station

367 Unjusan-ro, Jeondong-Myeon, Sejong City, Chungcheongnam-do

Jeonui Train Station

269-1 Eupnae-ri, Jeonui-myeon, Yeongi-gun, Chungcheongnam-do

Jochiwon Train Station

141 Won-ri, Jochiwon-eup, Yeongi-gun, Chungcheongnam-do

Maepo Train Station

414-5 Noho-ri, Buyong-myeon, Cheongwon-gun, Chungcheongbuk-do

Naepan Train Station

Dong-Myeon, Yeongi-Gun, Chungcheongnam-Do

Seochang Train Station
206-15 Sinan-ri, Jochiwon-eup, Yeongi-gun, Chungcheongnam-do

Sojeong-ri Train Station
Sojeong-ri, Sojeong-myeon, Yeongi-gun, Chungcheongnam-do

Seoul

Cheongnyangni Train Station
588-1 Jeonnong-dong, Dongdaemun-gu, Seoul

Oksu Train Station
75-3 Oksu-dong, Seongdong-gu, Seoul

Sangbong Train Station
100-14 Sangbong-dong, Jungnang-gu, Seoul

Seoul Train Station

43-205 Dongja-dong, Yongsan-gu, Seoul

Phone: + 82-2-1330, + 82-2-3149-2522, +82-2-3149-2530, +82-2-1544-7788, +82-2-1588-7788

Wangsimni Train Station

168-1 Haengdang-dong, Seongdong-gu, Seoul

Yeongdeungpo Train Station

618 Yeongdeungpo-dong, Yeongdeungpo-gu, Seoul

Yongsan Train Station

40-1 Hangangno 3(sam)-ga, Yongsan-gu, Seoul

Train Stations in Sri Lanka

Ahangama Train Station

Matara Road, Galle, Southern Province, Sri Lanka

Phone: 091-2283271

Ahungalle Train Station

Station Rd, Ahungalla, Sri Lanka

Akurala Train Station

Akurala, Galle, Southern Province, Sri Lanka

Alawwa Train Station

Alawwa-Maharagama Road, Alawwa, North Western Province, Sri Lanka

Phone: 037-2278171

Aluthgama Train Station

Station Access Rd, Aluthgama, Western Province, Sri Lanka

Phone: 034-2275282

Ambalangoda Train Station

Galle Road, Ambalangoda, Southern Province, Sri Lanka

Phone: 091-2258271

Ambepussa Train Station

Kandalama Road, Ambepussa, Western Province

Ambewela Train Station

World's End Road, Ambewela, Central Province, Sri Lanka

Phone: 052-2222114

Andadola Train Station

Berathuduwa Road, Balapitiya, Southern Province, Sri Lanka

Angampitiya Train Station

Meepe - Ingiriya Rd, Padukka, Sri Lanka

Angulana Train Station

Moratuwa, Western Province, Sri Lanka

Phone: 2605256

Anuradhapura Town Train Station

Railway Station, Sri Barathindra Mawatha, Anuradhapura, North Central Province, Sri Lanka

Anuradhapura Train Station

Jaya Sri Ma Bodhi Road

Phone: 025-2222271

Avisawella Train Station

Avissawella Rd, Avisawella, Sri Lanka

Phone: 036-2222271

Badulla Train Station

Station Rd., Badulla

Phone: 055-2222271

Balana Train Station

Kegalle, Sabaragamuwa Province, Sri Lanka

Balapitiya Train Station
Galle Rd, Southern Province, Sri Lanka
Phone: 091-2258446

Bambalapitiya Train Station
Bambalapitiya, Sri Lanka, Colombo 04
Phone: 2584503

Bandarawela Train Station
Beragala-Hali Ela Hwy, Bandarawela
Phone: 057-2222271

Bangadeniya Train Station
Peliyagoda-Puttalam Hwy, Bangadeniya
Phone: 032-2259570

Baseline Road Train Station
Dr. Danister De Silva Rd., Colombo, Western Province, Sri Lanka

Batuwatte Train Station

Ragama Batuwatta Rd., Batuwatta West

Bemmulla Train Station

Aluthgama-Wigoda Road, Gampaha, Western Province, Sri Lanka

Bentota Train Station

Station Access Rd, Bentota

Phone: 034-2275271

Beruwala Train Station

Hettimulla, Beruwala, Sri Lanka

Phone: 034-2276371

Bolawatta Train Station

Bolawatta Rd, Dankotuwa, Puttalam, North Western Province, Sri Lanka

Boossa Train Station

Galle Rd, Boossa, Sri Lanka

Borelessa Train Station

Station Rd, Puttalam, North Western
Province, Sri Lanka

Botale Train Station
Pirisyala-Bothale Rd, Gampaha, Western
Province, Sri Lanka

Bulugahagoda Train Station
Bulugahagoda Station Rd, Ja-Ela, Western
Province, Sri Lanka

Chilaw Train Station
Chilaw, North Western Province, Sri Lanka
Phone: 032-2222271

Cotta Road Train Station
Colombo, Western Province, Sri Lanka

Daraluwa Train Station
Daraluwa Station Rd, Gampaha, Western
Province, Sri Lanka

Dehiwala Train Station

Station Rd., Dehiwala-Mount Lavinia
Phone: 2713271

Dematagoda Train Station
Dr. Danister De Silva Rd., Dematagoda

Demodara Train Station
Badulla, Uva Province, Sri Lanka
Phone: 055-2294171

Deyatalawa Train Station
Diyatalawa Station Road, Diyathalawa, Uva
Province, Sri Lanka
Phone: 057-2229461

Dodanduwa Train Station
Galle Rd, Dodanduwa, Sri Lanka
Phone: 091-2264279

Ella Train Station
Ella Station Rd, Ella, Sri Lanka
Phone: 057-2228571

Enderamulla Train Station

Welikadamulla Road, Kelaniya

Fort Train Station

Olcott Mawatha Rd, Colombo, Western Province, Sri Lanka

Galboda Train Station

Galboda Rd, Galboda, Sri Lanka

Galgamuwa Train Station

Kurunegala road, Galgamuwa
Phone: 037-2253071

Galle Train Station

None Colombo Road
Phone: 091-2234945

Gampaha Train Station

Queen Mary's Rd, Gampaha, Western Province, Sri Lanka
Phone: 033-2222271

Gampola Train Station

Kandy Rd, Gampola, Sri Lanka

Phone: 081-2352271

Ganegoda Train Station

Gaspe Rd, Gampaha, Western Province, Sri Lanka

Ganemulla Train Station

Ganemulla, Western Province, Sri Lanka

Phone: 033-2260271

Gelioya Train Station

Kalugamuwa Rd, Gelioya, Sri Lanka

Ginthota Train Station

Galle, Southern Province, Sri Lanka

Phone: 091-2234272

Girambe Train Station

Wattegedara-Egalla-Puwakgahakotuwa Road, Kurunegala, North Western Province, Sri Lanka

Godagama Train Station
Godagama, Homagama, Sri Lanka

Great Western Train Station
Nuwara Eliya, Sri Lanka

Habaraduwa Train Station
Matara Rd, Habaraduwa, Sri Lanka

Haputale Train Station
Station Rd, Haputale, Sri Lanka
Phone: 052-2268071

Hatton Train Station
Hatton-Maskeliya-Dalhhousie Rd, Hatton, Central Province, Sri Lanka
Phone: 051-2222271

Heeloya Train Station

Badulla, Uva Province, Sri Lanka

Heendeniya Train Station
Gampaha, Western Province, Sri Lanka

Hettimulla Train Station
Beruwala, Western Province, Sri Lanka

Hikkaduwa Train Station
Galle Rd, Hikkaduwam, Sri Lanka
Phone: 091-2277271

Homagama Train Station
Denzil Kobbekaduwa Mawatha Rd,
Homagama, Sri Lanka
Phone: 2855290

Horape Train Station
Station Road, Welesara, Western Province,
Sri Lanka

Hunupitiya Train Station
Hunupitiya Road Station Road, Wattala

Phone: 2932271

Idalgasinna Train Station

Idalgashinna, Badulla, Uva Province, Sri Lanka

Ihala Watawala Train Station

Watawala, Central Province, Sri Lanka

Ihalakotte Train Station

Kegalle, Sabaragamuwa Province, Sri Lanka

Induruwa Train Station

Colombo-Galle-Hambantota-Wellawaya Highway, Galle, Southern Province, Sri Lanka

Phone: 034-2275500

Inguruoya Train Station

Inguruoya, Nawalapitiya, Central Province, Sri Lanka

Phone: 054-2223871

Jaela Train Station

Station Road, Ja-Ela, Sri Lanka

Phone: 2236409

Kadigamuwa Train Station

Kadigomuwa, Kegalle, Sri Lanka

Kadugannawa Train Station

Kadugannawa-Pottepitiya   Rd.,
Kadugannawa

Phone: 081-2571271

Kadugoda Train Station

Kadugoda, Colombo, Western Province, Sri Lanka

Kahawa Train Station

Galle Rd, Kahawa, Sri Lanka

Phone: 091-2258371

Kakkapalliya Train Station

Kakkapalliya, Puttalam, North Western Province, Sri Lanka

Kalutara North Train Station
Sri Sumangala North Rd, Kalutara, Wadduwa, Sri Lanka
Phone: 034-2232272

Kaluthara South Train Station
Station Rd, Kalutara, Sri Lanka
Phone: 034-2222271

Kamburugamuwa Train Station
Kamburugamuwa, Matara, Sri Lanka
Phone: 041-2222671

Kandana Train Station
Station Rd., Ja-Ela 11320, Western Province, Sri Lanka

Kandegoda Train Station
Thotawatta Rd, Kandegoda, Ambalangoda, Southern Province, Sri Lanka

Kandy Train Station
S W R D Bandaranaike Mawatha Rd, Kandy, Central Province, Sri Lanka
Phone: 081-2222271

Kattuwa Train Station
Kattuwa, Negombo, Western Province, Sri Lanka

Katugastota Train Station
Katugastota, Sri Lanka
Phone: 081-249971

Katugoda Train Station
Galle Rd, Katugoda, Southern Province, Sri Lanka

Katukurunda Train Station
Station Rd, Katukurunda, Kalutara, Sri Lanka

Katunayake Train Station

Railway St. Rd, Katunayake, Sri Lanka

Keenawala Train Station

Baduragoda-Kottala Rd, Keenawala, Gampaha, Western Province, Sri Lanka

Kelaniya Train Station

Station Road, Kelaniya, Peliyagoda 11600, Sri Lanka

Phone: 2911426

Kinigama Train Station

Kinigama, Bandarawela, Uva Province, Sri Lanka

Kirulapone Train Station

Kirulapone, Colombo, Western Province, Sri Lanka

Koggala Train Station

Matara Rd, Koggala, Sri Lanka

Kollupitiya Train Station
Kollupitiya, Colombo, Western Province, Sri Lanka
Phone: 2573229

Kosgama Train Station
Avissawella Rd, Kosgama, Sri Lanka

Kosgoda Train Station
Galle Rd, Kosgoda, Sri Lanka
Phone: 091-2264071

Koshinna Train Station
Koshinna, Kandy, Central Province, Sri Lanka

Kotagala Train Station
Kotagala Station Rd, Kotagala, Nuwara Eliya, Central Province, Sri Lanka
Phone: 051-2222439

Kottawa Train Station

Kottawa, Pannipitiya, Western Province, Sri Lanka

Phone: 2843494

Kudahakapola Train Station

Kudahakapola, Gampaha, Western Province, Sri Lanka

Kudawewa Train Station

Kudawewa, Puttalam, North Western Province, Sri Lanka

Kumarakanda Train Station

Galle Rd, Kumarakanda, Hikkaduwa, Southern Province, Sri Lanka

Kurunegala Train Station

Kurunegala Station Rd, Kurunegala 60000, Sri Lanka

Phone: 037-2222271

Liyanagemulla Train Station

Liyanagemulla, Katunayake, Western Province, Sri Lanka

Lunawa Train Station

Station Rd, Moratuwa 10400, Lunawa

Lunuwila Train Station

Lunuwila, Puttalam, North Western Province, Sri Lanka
Phone: 031-2255271

Madampagama Train Station

Galle Rd, Madampagama, Southern Province, Sri Lanka

Madampe Train Station

Bo Tree Rd, Madampe, Sri Lanka
Phone: 032-2247671

Madurankuliya Train Station

Madurankuliya, Peliyagoda-Puttalam Highway, Puttalam, North Western Province, Sri Lanka

Magelegoda Train Station
Magalegoda, Gampaha, Sri Lanka

Maggona Train Station
Galle Rd, Maggona, Sri Lanka

Maha Induruwa Train Station
Maha Induruwa, Colombo-Galle-Hambantota-Wellawaya Highway, Maha Induruwa, Southern Province, Sri Lanka

Mahaiyawa Train Station
B70, Kandy, Mahaiyawa, Central Province, Sri Lanka

Maharagama Train Station
Railway Rd, Maharagama, Western Province, Sri Lanka

Maho Train Station

Maho Yapahuwa Road, Maho

Phone: 037-2275271

Malapalla Train Station

Malapalla, Pannipitiya, Sri Lanka

Maradana Train Station

Dr. N. M. Perera Mawatha 218, Maradana

Phone: 2695722

Matale Train Station

Gongawella Rd, Matale, Central Province,
Sri Lanka

Phone: 066-2222271

Matara Train Station

Railway Station Rd, Matara, Southern
Province, Sri Lanka

Phone: 041-2222271

Meegoda Train Station

Meegoda, Colombo, Western Province, Sri Lanka

Midigama Train Station
Matara Rd, Midigama, Southern Province, Sri Lanka

Mihintale Train Station
Mihintale, Anuradhapura, North Central Province, Sri Lanka

Mihirigama Train Station
Pasyala-Giriulla Rd, Mirigama 11200, Sri Lanka
Phone: 033-2273271

Mirissa Train Station
Udupila Rd, Mirissa, Sri Lanka

Morakele Train Station
Morakele, Colombo, Sri Lanka

Moratuwa Train Station

Uswatta Lane 1, Moratuwa, Sri Lanka

Phone: 2645267

Mount Laviniya Train Station

Dehiwala-Mount Lavinia

Phone: 2712271

Mundel Train Station

Mundal, Puttalam, Sri Lanka

Nagollagama Train Station

Nagollagama, Kurunegala, North Western Province, Sri Lanka

Nailiya Train Station

Nailiya, Kurunegala, North Western Province, Sri Lanka

Nanuoya Train Station

Avissawella-Hatton-Nuwara Eliya Highway, Nuwara Eliya, Central Province, Sri Lanka

Phone: 052-2222873

Narahenpita Train Station

Narahenpita, Colombo, Western Province, Sri Lanka

Phone: 2582270

Nattandiya Train Station

Marawila-Udubaddawa Rd, Nattandiya, Sri Lanka

Phone: 032-2254271

Nawalapitiya Train Station

Nawalapitiya - Dolosbage Rd, Nawalapitiya, Sri Lanka

Phone: 054-2222271

Nawinna Train Station

Nawinna, Maharagama, Western Province, Sri Lanka

Negombo Train Station

Negombo, Western Province, Sri Lanka

Phone: 031-2222271

Nelumpokuna Train Station

Nelumpokuna, Madampe, North Western Province, Sri Lanka

Noor Nagar Train Station

Noor Nagar, Puttalam, North Western Province, Sri Lanka

Nugegoda Train Station

Station Ln, Nugegoda 10250, Sri Lanka
Phone: 2852626

Ohiya Train Station

Horton Plains National Park, Ohiya, Sri Lanka

Padukka Train Station

Padukka, Padukka, Western Province, Sri Lanka
Phone: 2859026

Palavi Train Station

Palavi, Puttalam, North Western Province, Sri Lanka
Phone: 032-2269371

Pallewela Train Station
Pallewela Station RD, Pallewela, Gampaha, Sri Lanka
Phone: 033-2273271

Panadura Train Station
Sagara Mawatha Rd, Panadura, Western Province, Sri Lanka
Phone: 038-2232271

Pannipitiya Train Station
Borella Rd, Pannipitiya, Sri Lanka

Parasangahawewa Train Station
Parasangahawewa, Anuradhapura, North Central Province, Sri Lanka

Pattipola Train Station

World's End Rd, Horton Plains National Park, Pattipola, Sri Lanka

Payagala North Train Station
Station Rd, Payagala, Katukurunda, Sri Lanka

Payagala south Train Station
Galle Rd, Payagala, Maggona, Sri Lanka
Phone: 034-2233760

Peradeniya Train Station
Peradeniya Road, Peradeniya
Phone: 081-2388271

Perakumpura Train Station
Perakumpura, Nuwara Eliya, Central Province, Sri Lanka

Peralanda Train Station
Peralanda Rd, Peralanda, Welesara, Sri Lanka

Periyanagavillu Train Station

Periyanagavillu, Puttalam, North Western Province, Sri Lanka

Pilimatalawa Train Station

Malgammana Rd, Pilimathalawa 20450, Sri Lanka

Pinwatta Train Station

Pinwatta Station Rd, Pinwatta, Panadura, Sri Lanka

Piyadigama Train Station

Kalegana Rd, Piyadigama, Galle, Sri Lanka

Polgahawela Train Station

Polgahawela-Kegalle Hwy. Kegalle Rd., Polgahawela

Phone: 037-2243271

Polwathumodara Train Station
Matara Road, Polwathumodara Weligama, Southern Province, Sri Lanka

Potuhera Train Station
Pothuhera, Kurunegala, North Western Province, Sri Lanka

Puttalam Train Station
Puttalam, North Western Province, Sri Lanka
Phone: 032-2265271

Radalla Train Station
Radalla, Nuwara Eliya, Sri Lanka

Ragama Train Station
Thewatta Rd, Ragama, Sri Lanka
Phone: 2959271

Rajgama Train Station
Galle Rd, Rathgama, Boossa, Sri Lanka

Rambukkana Train Station
Rambukkana-Katupitiya Rd., Rambukkana,
Sabaragamuwa Province, Sri Lanka
Phone: 035-2265271

Randenigama Train Station
Randenigama, Kurunegala, North Western
Province, Sri Lanka

Rathmalana Train Station
Rathmalana, Dehiwala-Mount Lavinia,
Western Province, Sri Lanka
Phone: 2635271

Richmond Hill Train Station
Richmond Hill, Richmond Kanda, Galle
80000, Sri Lanka

Saliyapura Train Station
Saliyapura, Anuradhapura, North Central
Province, Sri Lanka

Sarasavi Uyana Train Station

Sarasavi Uyana, Peradeniya, Sri Lanka

Phone: 081-2388282

Seeduwa Train Station

Seeduwa, Katunayake, Western Province,
Sri Lanka

Phone: 2253571

Senarathgama Train Station

Kurunegala Rd, Senarathgama,
Kurunegala, North Western Province, Sri
Lanka

Talawakele Train Station

A7 Tawalantenne - Talawakele Rd,
Talawakelle 22100, Sri Lanka

Phone: 052-2258271

Thalawa Train Station

Kurunegala Rd, Talawa, Sri Lanka

Thelwatta Train Station

Galle Rd, Telwatte, Sri Lanka

Tismalpola Train Station
Tismalpola, Kegalle, Sabaragamuwa Province, Sri Lanka

Tudella Train Station
Christ King Road, Tudella, Ja-Ela, Western Province, Sri Lanka

Uda Talawinna Train Station
Doragamuwa Rd, Uda Thalawinna, Kandy, Sri Lanka

Udahamulla Train Station
Udahamulla Station Rd, Udahamulla, Nugegoda, Sri Lanka

Uduwara Train Station
Uduwara, Badulla, Uva Province, Sri Lanka

Ukuwela Train Station

Railway Station Rd, B462, Ukuwela, Central Province, Sri Lanka
Phone: 066-2244527

Ulapane Train Station
Ulapane, Kandy, Sri Lanka
Phone: 081-2352671

Unawatuna Train Station
Heenatigala Rd, Unawatuna, Sri Lanka

Vavuniya Train Station
Goodshed Rd, Vavuniya, Sri Lanka
Phone: 024-2222271

Veyangoda Train Station
Station Rd, Veyangoda, Western Province, Sri Lanka
Phone: 033-2287271

Wadduwa Train Station
Wadduwa, Western Province, Sri Lanka
Phone: 038-2232571

Waga Train Station
Kaluaggala-Labugama Rd, Waga, Sri
Lanka
Phone: 036-2255271

Waikkala Train Station
Station Rd, Waikkala, Puttalam, North
Western Province, Sri Lanka

Walahapitiya Train Station
Walahapitiya, Puttalam, North Western
Province, Sri Lanka

Walgama Train Station
Welegoda Rd, Walgama, Matara, Sri
Lanka

Walpola Train Station
Walpola-Batuwatta Rd, Walpola, Welesara,
Western Province, Sri Lanka

Wanawasala Train Station

Korasawal Doowa Rd, Wanawasala, Wattala, Western Province, Sri Lanka

Watagoda Train Station
Tawalantenne - Talawakele Rd, Watagoda, Sri Lanka
Phone: 051-2236071

Watareka Train Station
Padukka Rd, Padukka, Watareka, Sri Lanka

Watawala Train Station
Avissawella-Hatton-Nuwara Eliya Hwy, Watawala, Sri Lanka
Phone: 051-2237271

Wattegama Train Station
Wattegama, Central Province, Sri Lanka
Phone: 081-2476271

Wellawa Train Station

Hiripitiya Road, Wellawa, Sri Lanka

Wellawatta Train Station

Wellawatta South, Colombo, Sri Lanka

Phone: 2585875

Wijaya Rajadahana Train Station

Pasyala-Giriulla Rd, Wijaya Rajadahana, Gampaha, Western Province, Sri Lanka

Yagoda Train Station

Weera Mawatha, Ganemulla, Western Province, Sri Lanka

Yatagama Train Station

Yatagama, Rambukkana, Sri Lanka

Train Stations in Syria

Aleppo Train Station
Gare de Baghdad district, Aleppo

Al-Qamishli Train Station
Al Qamishli, Al Hasakah, Syria

Ar Ra'i Train Station
Çobanbey, Ar Ra'i, Syria

Ar-Raqqah Train Station
Ar Raqqah, Ar-Raqqah Governorate, Syria

Damascus Train Station
Al Hijaz Train Station, Sa'adalah El-Jabri, Damascus, Syria

Homs Train Station
Al Korniche St, Homs, Homs Governorate, Syria

Latakia Train Station

Latakia, Syria

Tall Rifat Train Station

Tall Rifat, Aleppo Governorate, Syria

Tartus Train Station

Tartus, Tartus Governorate, Syria

Train Stations in Taiwan

Baifu Train Station
Qidu District, Keelung City, Taiwan
Phone: +886-2-24528372

Baishatun Train Station
Tongxiao Township, Miaoli County, Taiwan
Phone: +886-3-7793066

Banqiao Train Station
B1F, No. 5, Zhanqian Rd., Banqiao
District, New Taipei, Taiwan
Phone: +886-2-89691036

Beihu Train Station
Taoyuan County, Taiwan
Phone: +886-3-5993850

Beipu Train Station
Xincheng Township, Hualien County,
Taiwan

Phone: +886-3-8263809

Chang Jung Christian University(CJCU) Train Station
Guiren District, Tainan, Taiwan
Phone: +886-6-2782615

Changhua(Zhanghua) Train Station
Changhua City, Changhua County, Taiwan
Phone: +886-4-7274218

Checheng Train Station
Checheng, Shuili Township, Nantou County, Taiwan
Phone: +886-49-2774749

Chenggong Train Station
Wuri District, Taichung, Taiwan
Phone: +886-4-23371986

Chiayi(Jiayi) Train Station
West District, Chiayi City, Taiwan
Phone: +886-5-2228904

Chongde Train Station

Xiulin Township, Hualien County, Taiwan

Phone: +886-3-8621365

Dacun Train Station

Dacun Township, Changhua County, Taiwan

Phone: +886-4-8525148

Dadu Train Station

Dadu District, Taichung, Taiwan

Phone: +886-4-26992523

Dahu Train Station

No. 24, Tiānyòu Rd, Dahu Train Station, Luzhu District, Kaohsiung City, Taiwan

Phone: +886-7-6932127

Dajia Train Station

Dajia District, Taichung, Taiwan

Phone: +886-4-26872022

Dali Train Station

No. 326, Sec. 6, Binhai Rd., Dali Village, Toucheng Township, Yilan County

Phone: +886-3-9781171

Dalin Train Station

No. 2, Zhōngshān Road, Dalin Township, Chiayi City, Taiwan

Phone: +886-5-2654804

Daqiao Train Station

No. 835號, Zhōnghuá Road, Yongkang District, Tainan City, Taiwan

Phone: +886-6-3021755

Daqing Train Station

South District, Taichung, Taiwan

Phone: +886-4-22637940

Dasi Train Station

No. 63, Sec. 5, Binhai Rd., Dasi Village, Toucheng Township, Yilan County

Dong'ao Train Station
No. 1, Dongyue Village, Nanao Township,Yilan County
Phone: +886-3-9986053

Dongshan Train Station
No. 1, Jhongjheng Rd., Dongshan Village, Dongshan Township, Yilan County
Phone: +886-3-9594221

Douliu Train Station
640, Taiwan, Yunlin County, Douliu City
Phone: +886-5-5332900

Dounan Train Station
No.2, Zhongshan Rd., Dounan Township, Yunlin County 630, Taiwan
Phone: +886-5-5972039

Erjie Train Station
No.37, Fusing Central Rd., Wujie Township, Yilan County 268, Taiwan
Phone: +886-3-9650304

Ershui Train Station
Nantou County, Nantou City, Taiwan
Phone: +886-4-8792027

Fangliao Train Station
Fangliao Township, Pingtung County, Taiwan
Phone: +886-8-8782041

Fengshan Train Station
Fongshan District, Kaohsiung City, Taiwan
Phone: +886-7-7460423

Fengyuan Train Station
Fengyuan District, Taichung, Taiwan
Phone: +886-4-25207950

Fulong Train Station
No. 2, Fulong St., Fulong Village, Gongliao District, New Taipei City
Phone: +886-2-24991800

Gangshan Train Station

Gangshan District, Kaohsiung, Taiwan

Phone: +886-7-6212074

Gongliao Train Station

No. 33, Chaoyang St., Gongliao Village, Gongliao District, New Taipei City

Phone: +886-2-24941500

Guishan Train Station

No. 261, Sec. 3, Binhai Rd., Gengsin Village, Toucheng Township, Yilan County

Phone: +886-3-9770351

Guzhuang Train Station

Dawu Township, Taitung County, Taiwan

Phone: +886-8-9791820

Hanben Train Station

No. 56, Sec. 1, Suhua Rd., Aohua Village , Nanao Township, Yilan County

Phone: +886-3-9985238

Heren Train Station
Hualien County, Taiwan
Phone: +886-3-8681221

Houbi Train Station
Houbi District, Tainan, Taiwan
Phone: +886-5-6872055

Houli Train Station
Houli District, Taichung City, Taiwan 421
Phone: +886-4-25562038

Houlong Train Station
Houlong Township, Miaoli County, Taiwan
Phone: +886-3-7728616

Houtong Train Station
No. 70, Chailiao Rd., Guangfu Village,
Ruifang District, New Taipei City
Phone: +886-2-24977747

Houzhuang Train Station

Daliao District, Kaohsiung City, Taiwan

Phone: +886-7-7020149

Hsinchu(Xinzhu) Train Station

Hsinchu City, Taiwan

Phone: +886-3-5237441

Hualien Port Train Station

Hualien City, Hualien County, Taiwan

Phone: +886-3-8222468

Huatan Train Station

Huatan Township, Changhua County, Taiwan

Phone: +886-4-7881418

Jiabei Train Station

East District, Chiayi City, Taiwan

Phone: +886-5-2334584

Jialu Train Station

Fangshan Township, Pingtung County, Taiwan

Phone: +886-8-8720791

Jiaoxi Train Station

No. 1, Wuncyuan Rd., Deyang Village, Jiaosi Township, Yilan County

Phone: +886-3-9886940

Jiji Train Station

No.75, Minsheng Rd., Jiji Township, Nantou County 552, Taiwan

Phone: +886-49-2762546

Kangle Train Station

Taitung City, Taitung County, Taiwan

Phone: +886-8-9383107

Kaohsiung(Gaoxiong) Train Station

318 Chien Kuo 2nd Road, Kaohsiung, Taiwan

Phone: +886-7-2371507

Phone: +886-7-2352376

Keelung(Jilong) Train Station
No. 1, Gangxi St., Ren-ai District, Keelung
City, Taiwan
Phone: +886-2-24263743

Linnei Train Station
Linnei Township, Yunlin County, Taiwan
Phone: +886-5-5892040

Longjing Train Station
Longjing District, Taichung, Taiwan
Phone: +886-4-26355578

Luodong Train Station
No. 2, Gongjheng Rd., Dasin Village,
Luodong Township, Yilan County
Phone: +886-3-9542117

Luzhu Train Station
Luzhu District, Kaohsiung, Taiwan
Phone: +886-7-6072723

Miaoli Train Station
Weigong Rd., No. 1, Miaoli City, Miaoli County, Taiwan
Phone: +886-3-7260031

Minxiong Train Station
Minxiong Township, Chiayi County, Taiwan
Phone: +886-5-2264272

Mudan Train Station
No. 159, Mudan Rd., Shuangxi District, New Taipei City

Nan'ao Train Station
No. 22, Datong Rd., Nanciang Village, Su-ao Township, Yilan County
Phone: +886-3-9981971

Nangang Train Station
No. 380, Sec.7, Zhongxiao E. Rd., Nangang, Taipei, Taiwan
Phone: +886-2-27838645

Nanke Train Station

Xinshi District, Tainan City, Taiwan

Phone: +886-6-5896356

Neili Train Station

Zhonghua Rd., Sec. 1, No. 267, Zhongli, Taoyuan County, Taiwan

Phone: +886-3-4559725

Pingtung(Pingdong) Train Station

Pingtung City, Pingtung County, Taiwan

Phone: +886-8-7322450

Puxin Train Station

Yangmei City, Taoyuan County, Taiwan

Phone: +886-3-4827100

Qiaotou Train Station

Qiaotou District, Kaohsiung City, Taiwan

Phone: +886-7-6115424

Qidu Train Station

Qidu District, Keelung City, Taiwan
Phone: +886-2-24553426

Qingshui Train Station

Qingshui District, Taichung, Taiwan
Phone: +886-4-26222021

Ruifang Train Station

No. 82, Sec. 3, Mingdeng Rd., Longtan Village, Ruifang District, New Taipei City
Phone: +886-2-24972033

Sandiaoling Train Station

No. 1, Yuliao Rd., Shihren Village, Ruifang District, New Taipei City
Phone: +886-2-24977896

Sankeng Train Station

Ren'ai District, Keelung City, Taiwan
Phone: +886-2-24230289

Sanyi Train Station

Sanyi Township, Miaoli County, Taiwan

Phone: +886-3-7874763

Shalu Train Station
Shalu District, Taichung, Taiwan
Phone: +886-4-26625057

Shalun Train Station
Guiren District, Tainan City, Taiwan
Phone: +886-6-3032686

Shanjia Train Station
No. 28, Shanjia Street, Shulin District, New Taipei City
Phone: +886-2-26808874

Shihcheng Train Station
No. 230, Sec. 7, Binhai Rd., Shihcheng Village, Toucheng Township, Yilan County

Shuangxi Train Station
No. 1, Chaoyang St., Sinji Village, Shuangxi District, New Taipei City
Phone: +886-2-24932980

Shuili Train Station

Shueili Township, Nantou County, Taiwan

Phone: +886-49-2770015

Shulin Train Station

Shulin District, New Taipei City, Taiwan

Phone: +886-2-26812052

Sicheng Train Station

No. 24, Jhancian Rd., Wusha Village, Jiaosi Township, Yilan County

Phone: +886-3-9282449

Sijiaoting Train Station

Ruifang District, New Taipei, Taiwan

Phone: +886-2-24579346

Songshan Train Station

Songshan District, Taipei, Taiwan

Phone: +886-2-27673819

Su'ao Train Station

No. 1, Taiping Rd., Sunan Village, Su-ao Township, Yilan County

Phone: +886-3-9962028

Su'aoxin Train Station

No. 238-1, Sec. 2, Jhongshan Rd., Su-ao Township, Yilan County

Phone: +886-3-9961004

Taichung Port Train Station

Qingshui District, Taichung, Taiwan

Phone: +886-4-26225374

Taichung(Taizhong) Train Station

Central District, Taichung City, Taiwan

Phone: +886-4-22227236

Tainan Train Station

Beimen Rd., Sec. 2, No. 4, East District, Tainan, Taiwan

Phone: +886-6-2261314

Taipei Train Station

No. 3, Beiping W. Rd., Zhongzheng District, Taipei City (East of the Main Hall at 1F)
Phone: +886-2-2312-3256

Taitung(Taidong) Train Station

Taitung City, Taitung County, Taiwan
Phone: +886-8-9229687

Tanzi Train Station

Tanzi District, Taichung City, Taiwan
Phone: +886-4-25319200

Taoyuan Train Station

Taoyuan City, Taoyuan County, Taiwan
Phone: +886-3-3323304

Tianzhong Train Station

Tianzhong Township, Changhua County, Taiwan
Phone: +886-4-8742142

Tongluo Train Station

Tongluo Township, Miaoli County, Taiwan

Phone: +886-3-7983838

Tongxiao Train Station

Tongxiao Township, Miaoli County, Taiwan

Phone: +886-3-7758300

Toucheng Train Station

Toucheng Township, Yilan County, Taiwan

Phone: +886-3-9771429

Waiao Train Station

No. 217, Sec. 2, Binhai Rd., Waiao Village, Toucheng Township, Yilan County

Wanhua Train Station

Wanhua District, Taipei, Taiwan

Phone: +886-2-23020481

Wudu Train Station

Xizhi District, New Taipei, Taiwan

Phone: +886-2-86472000

Wuri Train Station
Wuri District, Taichung, Taiwan
Phone: +886-4-23381071

Xike Train Station
Xizhi District, New Taipei, Taiwan
Phone: +886-2-23815226#8730

Xincheng Train Station
Xincheng Township, Hualien County, Taiwan
Phone: +886-3-8611237

Xinwuri Train Station
Wuri District, Taichung City, Taiwan
Phone: +886-4-23376883

Xinying Train Station
Xinying District, Tainan City, Taiwan
Phone: +886-6-6322104

Xinzuoying Train Station

Zuoying District, Kaohsiung, Taiwan

Phone: +886-7-5887825

Xizhi Train Station

Xizhi District, New Taipei, Taiwan

Phone: +886-2-26415096

Yangmei Train Station

Yangmei City, Taoyuan County, Taiwan

Phone: +886-3-4782893

Yilan Train Station

No. 1, Guangfu Rd., Hemu Village , Yilan
City, Yilan County

Phone: +886-3-9323801

Yingge Train Station

Yingge District, New Taipei, Taiwan

Phone: +886-2-26792004

Yongkang Train Station

No.459, Zhongshan Rd.,Puyuan Village,Yongkang City, Tainan County 710, Taiwan

Phone: +886-6-2323305

Yongle Train Station

No. 148, Yongle S. Rd., Yongle Village, Su-ao Township, Yilan County

Phone: +886-3-9961889

Yuanli Train Station

Yuanli Township, Miaoli County, Taiwan

Phone: +886-3-7851013

Yuanlin Train Station

Yuanlin Township, Changhua County, Taiwan

Phone: +886-4-8320544

Yuli Train Station

No. 39號, Kānglè St, Yuli Township, Hualien County, Taiwan 981

Phone: +886-3-8882020

Zhiben Train Station
950, Taiwan, Taitung County, Taitung City
Phone: +886-8-9514482

Zhixue Train Station
No. 1號, Zhōngzhèng Rd, Shoufeng Township, Hualien County, Taiwan 974
Phone: +886-3-8662966

Zhongli Train Station
No. 139, Zhonghe Rd., Zhongli, Taoyuan County, Taiwan
Phone: +886-3-4223235

Zhongzhou Train Station
Rende District, Tainan City, Taiwan
Phone: +886-6-2667191

Zhudong Train Station
No. 196, Donglin Rd., Jilin Village, Zhudong Township, Hsinchu County

Phone: +886-3-5962042

Zhuifen Train Station
Dadu District, Taichung, Taiwan
Phone: +886-4-26933106

Zhunan Train Station
Zhonghua Rd., Sec. 1, No. 267, Zhunan
Township, Miaoli County, Taiwan
Phone: +886-3-7472030

Train Stations in Tajikistan

Dushanbe Train Station
Rudaki Ave. 35, Dushanbe 734012, Tajikistan

Kulob Train Station
Kulyab, Kulob, Tajikistan

Vahdat Train Station
Yangi Bosor, Vahdat, Districts of Republican Subordination, Tajikistan

Yovon Train Station
Yovon, Khatlon, Tajikistan

Train Stations in Thailand
Northern Line

Bang Sue Junction Train Station
Rotfai 1 Alley, Bang Sue District
Phone: 02 587 4613; 02 222 0175

Ayutthaya Train Station
Ho Rattanachai Ayutthaya
Phone: 035 241 521

Ban Phachi Junction Train Station
Phachi Subdistrict, Phachi Municipality,
Ayutthaya

Lop Buri Train Station
Naphrakan Road, Tha Hin Subdistrict, Lop
Buri City, Lop Buri
Phone: 036 411 022

Nakhon Sawan Train Station

National Road No.3001, Nong Pling Subdistrict, Nakhon Sawan City, Nakhon Sawan

Phichit Train Station
Fang Sathani Rotfai Road, Nai Muang Subdistrict, Phichit City

Phitsanulok Train Station
Bung Phra Road, Nai Muang Subdistrict, Phitsanulok City
Phone: 055 258 005

Ban Dara Junction Train Station
Ban Dara Subdistrict, Phichai District, Uttaradit

Sawankhalok Train Station
Chrotwithithong Road, Muang Sawankhalok Subdistrict, Sawankhalok District

Uttaradit Train Station

Samranruen Road, Tha It Subdistrict, Uttaradit City

Sila At Train Station
National Highway No.1045, Tha Pla Subdistrict, Uttaradit City

Den Chai Train Station
Den Chai Subdistrict, Den Chai District, Phrae 54110

Nakhon Lampang Train Station
Sop Tui, Mueang Lampang District, Lampang 52100

Khun Tan Train Station
Khun Tan, Lampang, Thailand

Lamphun Train Station
Lamphun, Lamphun District, Thailand

Lampang Train Station

Sop Tui, Lampang
Phone: 054 217 026; 054 217 024

Chiang Mai Train Station
Charoen Muang Rd., Wat Ket, Muang
Chiang Mai, Chiang Mai 50000
Phone: 053 236 094; 053 245 363

Northeastern Line

Saraburi Train Station
Mueang Saraburi District, Saraburi 18000

Kaeng Khoi Junction Train Station
Kaeng Khoi District, Saraburi

Pak Chong Train Station
Pak Chong District, Nakhon Ratchasima
30130

Nakhon Ratchasima Train Station
Mukkhamontri Rd, Nai Muang, Muang,
Nakhon Ratchasima, 30000

Phone: 044 242 044

Thanon Chira Junction Train Station
Watcharasarit Rd, Nai Mueang, Mueang, Nakhon Ratchasima, 30000

Buri Ram Train Station
Niwas Rd, Nai Muang, Muang, Buriram, 31000

Surin Train Station
Nai Mueang, Surin

Si Sa Ket Train Station
Ratchakan Rotfai 3 Rd, Mueang Si Sa Ket District, Si Sa Ket 33000
Phone: 045 611 525

Ubon Ratchathani Train Station
Soi Yooyen Rd, Warin Chamrap District, Ubon Ratchathani 34190
Phone: 045 321 004

Lam Narai Train Station
Chai Badan District, Lopburi

Chatturat Train Station
Chatturat District, Ban Kok Chaiyaphum 36130

Bua Yai Junction Train Station
Kanrotfai Rd, Bua Yai, Bua Yai, Nakhon Ratchasima, 30120

Khon Kaen Train Station
Nai Mueang Khon Kaen District, Khon Kaen

Udon Thani Train Station
Prajak Road, Mueang Udon Thani District, Udon Thani
Phone: 02 222 0175

Nong Khai Train Station

Mueang Nong Khai District, Nong Khai

Lak Si Train Station

Talat Bang Khen, Lak Si Bangkok

Phone: 02 573 1394; 02 222 0175

Southern Line

Bang Sue Junction Train Station

Thoet Damri Road, Chatuchak, Chatuchak District, Bangkok

Bang Bamru Train Station

Soi Sirinthorn 4, Bang Phlat Subdistrict, Bang Phlat District, Bangkok (Mainline Station)

Taling Chan Junction Train Station

Taling Chan, Bangkok

Thon Buri Train Station

Thanon Sutthawat Rd, Siriraj, Bangkok Noi, Bangkok 10700
Phone: 02 222 0175

Salaya Train Station

Phutthamonthon District, Nakhon Pathom 73170

Nakhon Pathom Train Station

Langsa Thanee Rodfai Road, Nakhon Pathom, Mueang Nakhon Pathom District, Nakhon Pathom 73000
Phone: 034 242 305

Nong Pladuk Junction Train Station

Ban Pong District, Ratchaburi 70110

Ban Pong Train Station

Ban Pong District, Ratchaburi

Ratchaburi Train Station

Mueang Ratchaburi District, Ratchaburi 70000

Phetchaburi Train Station

Rotfai Road, Mueang Phetchaburi District, Phetchaburi 76000

Phone: 032 425 211

Hua Hin Train Station

Hua Hin 61 Alley, Hua Hin District, Prachuap Khiri Khan

Phone: 032 511 073

Wang Phong Train Station

Pran Buri District, Prachuap Khiri Khan

Pran Buri Train Station

Pran Buri District, Prachuap Khiri Khan 77120

Prachuap Khiri Khan Train Station

54 Maharat Road, Mueang Prachuap Khiri Khan District, Prachuap Khiri Khan

Phone: 032 611 175

Bang Saphan Yai Train Station

Kamnoet Nopphakhun, Bang Saphan, Prachuap Khiri Khan 77140

Phone: 032 691 552

Chumphon Train Station

Krumluang Chumphon Road, Mueang Chumphon District, Chumphon

Phone: 077 511 103

Lang Suan Train Station

Lang Suan District, Chumphon 86110

Ban Thung Pho Junction Train Station

Phunphin District, Surat Thani

Surat Thani Train Station

Tha Kham, Phunphin District, Surat Thani 84130

Phone: 077 311213

Thung Song Junction Train Station

Thung Song District, Nakhon Si Thammarat 80110

Trang Train Station
Sathani Alley, Mueang Trang District, Trang
Phone: 075 218 012

Kantang Train Station
Kantang District, Trang 92110

Khao Chum Thong Junction Train Station
Khao Chum Thong, Chulabhorn, Nakhon Si Thammarat 80130

Nakhon Si Thammarat Train Station
Tha Wang, Mueang Nakhon Si Thammarat District, Nakhon Si Thammarat 80000

Patthalung Train Station
Muang Phatthalung District, Phatthalung 93000

Hat Yai Junction Train Station

Rotfai Road, Hat Yai Subdistrict, Hat Yai City, Songkhla

Phone: 074 243 705; 074 238 005

Pattani Train Station

Khok Pho District, Pattani 94120

Yala Train Station

Mueang Yala District, Yala

Cha-Am Train Station

Narathip Road, Cha Am

Phone: 032 471 159

Don Muang Train Station

Si Kan, Don Mueang, 10210 Bangkok

Phone: 02 566 2957; 02 222 0175

Namtok Branch

Kanchanaburi Train Station

Saeng Chuto Road, Mueang Kanchanaburi District, Kanchanaburi

Phone: 034 511 285

Nam Tok Train Station
Sai Yok District, Kanchanaburi

Eastern Line

Makkasan Train Station
Nikhom Makkasan, Ratchathewi, Bangkok

Hua Mak Train Station
Suan Luang District, Bangkok

Hua Ta Khe Train Station
Lat Krabang, Bangkok

Chachoengsao Junction Train Station
Mueang Chachoengsao District, Chachoengsao

Khlong Sip Kao Junction Train Station

Bang Nam Priao District, Chachoengsao

Aranyaprathet Train Station

Aranyaprathet District, Sa Kaeo

Si Racha Junction Train Station

Surasak, Si Racha District, Chon Buri
20110

Khao Chi Chan Junction Train Station

Sattahip District, Chon Buri 20250

Ban Phlu Ta Luang Train Station

Sattahip District, Chon Buri

Pattaya Train Station

45 Sukhumvit Road Pattaya
Phone: 038 429 285

Maekong Line

Wongwian Yai Train Station

Bang Yi Ruea, Thon Buri, Bangkok 10600

Talat Phlu Train Station
Talat Phlu, Thon Buri, Bangkok 10600

Wat Sai Train Station
Ekkachai, Bang Khun Thian, Chom Thong,
Bangkok 10150

Maha Chai Train Station
Mueang Samut Sakhon District, Samut
Sakhon

Tha Chin River

Ban LaemTrain Station
Mueang Samut Sakhon District, Samut
Sakhon

Mae KlongTrain Station
Mueang Samut Songkhram District, Samut
Songkhram

Bangkok

Bangkok Hua Lamphong Train Station

Rama IV Rd, Pathum Wan, Bangkok, 10330

Train Stations in Turkmenistan

Ashgabat Train Station

Ashgabat, Ahal, Turkmenistan

Turkmenbashi Train Station

Turkmenbashi, Balkan, Turkmenistan

Train Stations in Uzbekistan

Tashkent Train Station

Tashkent-Central Station, 7, Turkestan Street, Tashkent

Phone: +(99871) 299 72 16, 1005

Bukhara Train Station

Phone: +(99865) 524 65 93

Samarkand Train Station

3, Beruniy Street, Samarkand

Phone: +(99866) 229 15 32

Urgench Train Station

Urgench, Uzbekistan

Termez Train Station

1, Ibn Sino Street, Termez

Phone: +(99876)2222335

Phone: +(99876)2222393

Karshi Train Station

Karshi, Qarshi, Uzbekistan

Navoi Train Station
Ravshanov Street , Navoi
Phone: +(998436) 225 59 07

Kokand Train Station
11, Shoxruxobod Street , Kokand
Phone: +(99873) 552 33 93
Phone: +(99873) 552 38 12
Phone: +(99873) 552 39 46

Nukus Train Station
Dosnazarov Street, Nukus
Phone: +(99861) 223 29 52

Chirchik Train Station
Boz-Su Street, Chirchik
Phone: +(99871)7193518

Andizhan Train Station
2, Amir Temur Street, Andizhan
Phone: +(99874)2922260

Phone: +(99874)2242170

Jizzakh Train Station
1, N.Kushakov Street, Jizzakh
Phone: +(99872)2223980
Phone: +(99872)2223990

Kagan Train Station
3, Umid Street, Kagan
Phone: +(99865)5247325
Phone: +(99865)5247332

Margilan Train Station
1, Mashrab Street, Margilan
Phone: +(99873)2375728

Namangan Train Station
58, Amir Temur Street, Namangan
Phone: +(99869)2334294

Fergana Train Station
1, Mashrab Street, Fergana
Phone: +(99873)2371544

Phone: +(99873)2375728

Yangiyul Train Station (Tashkent reg.)
1, Privokzalnaya Street, Yangiyul
Phone: +(99871)6022487

Train Stations in Vietnam

Binh Dinh Train Station

Van Hoi 2, Dieu Tri Town, Tuy Phuoc District, Binh Dinh Province

Phone: +84-56 3833 255 / 3833 249

Da nang Train Station

No. 202, Hai Phong Str, Da Nang City

Phone: +84 511 3821 175 /+84 511 3823 810

Dalat Train Station

Nguyen Trai Street, Ward 9 Dalat city, Dalat 61000, Vietnam

Phone: 0903640643

Danang Train Station

200 Hai Phong street , Thanh Khe District , Da Nang City

Dieu Tri Train Station

1A Dieu Tri , Quy Nhon City, Binh Dinh Province

Dong Ha City Train Station
No. 02 Le Thanh Ton Street, Dong Ha City, Quang Tri Province
Phone: 053-3850-631 - Fax: 053-3859-134

Dong Hoi Train Station
Sub-regional 4, Nam Ly District, Dong Hoi City, Quang Binh Province

Hai Phong Train Station
75 Luong Khanh Thien street, Ngo Quyen district, Hai Phong city.

Hanoi Train Station
120 Le Duan Str, Cua Nam Ward, Hoan Kiem Dist, Hanoi
Phone: +84 4 3 9423 697

Ho Chi Minh City Train Station

Saigon Train Station, No. 1, Nguyen Thong Str, 9 Ward, Dist 3, Ho Chi Minh City

Phone: +84 8343 6528 / +84 8346 6091

Hue Train Station

No. 2, Bui Thi Xuan Str, Hue City

Phone: +84 54 3822 175

Muong Man Train Station

Muong Man commune, Ham Thuan Nam district, Binh Thuan province

Nam Dinh Train Station

2 Tran Dang Ninh, Nam Dinh City

Phone: +84 350 3836558 - Fax: +84 350 3865756

Nghe An Train Station

No. 1, Le Ninh Road, Vinh City, Nghe An

Phone: 038-3853-426 - Fax: 038-3853-426

Nha Trang Train Station

17 Thai Nguyen Street, Phuoc Tan Ward, Nha Trang City

Phone: +84 583 822 113

Ninh Binh Train Station

No. 1 Hoang Hoa Tham Road, Than District, Ninh Binh City

Phone: 030.3673.619 - Fax: 030.3881.385

Phu Ly City Train Station

National Highway 1A, Hai Ba Trung District, Phu Ly City, Ha Nam Province

Phone: +84 0351 3 852168

Quang Binh Train Station

Sub-regional 4 (Tiểu Khu 4), Nam Ly District, Dong Hoi City, Quang Binh

Phone: 052-3820-558 - Fax: 052-3837-429

Thanh Hoa Train Station

No. 2, Dinh Nghe Street, Thanh Hoa City

Phone: 037.3851.527 - Fax: 037.3757.236

Thap Cham Train Station
7 Phan Dinh Phung, My Hung Ward, Phan
Rang Commune, Ninh Thuan Province

Tuy Hoa Train Station
146 Le Trung Kien street , Tuy Hoa city ,
Phu Yen Province

Vinh Train Station
No 1 - Le Ninh street, Quan Bau Ward,
Vinh City, Nghe An Province.

Conclusion

Visit J. Doyle White's author page on Amazon for a listing of all his books, including *The Ultimate North America Train Travel Guide*, *The Ultimate Europe Train Travel Guide*, and *The Top 10 Romantic Train Destinations of the USA*.

Visit his website www.BlueMarbleXpress.com.

J. DOYLE WHITE

Made in United States
North Haven, CT
13 December 2021

12606457R10326